THE WEIGHTED FEATHER
VOL. 2

First Paperback Edition April 2024
Cover Design by Julie Hightman
Edited by Julie Hightman

ISBN: 979-8-9875860-2-0 (Paperback)
ISBN: 979-8-9875860-3-7 (ebook)
Library of Congress Control Number: 2022908492

Published by Julie Hightman
www.faizhealing.net/books
Portland, OR, USA

THE WEIGHTED FEATHER VOL. 2

Essays for Alchemical Living & Empowering Mindfulness

JULIE J. HIGHTMAN

Julie J. Hightman

"This book is dedicated to all those I have shared life with and witnessed in the journey of expanding mindfulness. Thank you for your love, laughter, tears, and wisdom."

Contents

A Letter from the Author

      This book was written for the minds and hearts of individuals seeking mindfulness and provocative considerations that support them in their intentions for holistic fulfillment. The essays in this book open a journey into self-awareness and refine questions and perceptions one is cultivating or reviewing. Each concept is like an oyster bed filled with many pearls. My advice as the author is to take your time when drinking in the thoughts. Meditate on what resonates. This means reflecting in what already aligns in the perceptions of self, behaviors, and experiences as well as what feels harder to grasp, accept, or offer consideration to.

      All emotions and thoughts are valid because they appear as a guidelight to seeing deeper connections within one's personal associations to the narrative they have experienced, are actively living, and intend to create. The origin of truth is always found within once we refine the path to unfold it. The closer we are to this sense of truth that aligns in the core of self, the more we trust ourselves to make choices that lead to more fulfilling outcomes. This is the path of sovereignty. It is the journey of becoming the authentic self in harmonious balance with our relationships to "other" in the world.

      Building loyalty with the authentic self supports the integrity and skills we have the capacity to embody. Integrity requires consistent honesty and accountability with self and others.

One may aspire or idealize about self in the mind but authentic truths only endure when choices and behaviors reveal actualized integrity and embodiment of them. Embracing vulnerability and giving oneself permission to deepen understanding in the fabric of emotions and thoughts interconnecting bestows clarity in how one is designed. This clarity establishes opportunity for healthy autonomy, which potentiates the strength to be seen by others honoring their own integrity for mutual exchange.

How do you want to live life? How do you want to perceive yourself when you reflect on your choices in life as a legacy? The experiences of life offer us many paths of transformation. Cyclical patterns that are learned and witnessed may subject one to a sense of impotence. They may also be shifted, released, and redesigned when one aspires to the release of karma and the cultivation of alchemy within.

May the passion in your blood, the wisdom in your bones, and the illumination of your essence be your closest allies in the navigation of your own personal narrative.

May the passages in these pages open the door to the vast networks of mindful living and support you in the more graceful acquisitions of holistic fulfillment for your incarnate soul.

In Harmony,
Julie J Hightman

Introduction: Becoming the Authentic Self

In Egyptian lore, Anubis, the God of the Dead stands at the gateway to the spirit world with his scales to weigh the soul. The scale of souls is balanced by the weight of a feather to assess the lightness a soul has attained. The degree of light attained in one's being is dependent on the integrity and truth they embody in alignment with their authentic self. The vibrational purity of this authentic self resonates in every circumstance throughout the journey of a life to activate and influence the cultivation of en-lighten-ment. This path of enlightenment unveils the keys to personal empowerment, release from karmic bondage, and profound wisdom in the connectivity of all things.

The word enlightenment represents the concept of finding lightness in the meaning of self and the meaning of life. Harnessing the potency of this lightness is achieved within the alchemy of suffering and healing, of creation and death, of the known and the unknown. The expansion of awareness may be constructed in many ways. That is why the sages speak of "1000-fold" or "infinite" paths to reaching enlightenment. These paths have many peaks and valleys with frequent diverging and converging crossroads. Every soul comes into body with their own unique design that aligns them to the core programs of their own authentic self, as well as the threads in the vast fabric of the universal authentic self. In the warp and weft of the individual and universal authenticity, the offerings of harmony and fulfillment are defined. Peeling back the layers of perception and unwinding the threads reveals the solid or hollow core of truth, including the operable value of its structure when intact.

Alchemy is a physical and meta-physical process. Billions of atoms dance in and out of time and space to form, to merge, to bond, and to transform in the creation of matter, as we know it. What is matter? What does it matter? Matter is meaning and a lack of meaning, waiting to be perceived. All thoughts, emotions, and actions represent what "matter" is within and how "what matters" is directed or contained for use in our internal and external world of experience. The natural process of existence is alchemical. This includes the path of humanity and the path of the soul. Acknowledging and embracing the opportunity to engage in the alchemy of life, by choice, further inspires curiosity and enthusiasm for the magic in the mystery we all feel deep within. Even without acknowledgment, the alchemical synchrony of one's path persists beneath the veils of awareness. This inherent truth of the authentic self is always present and interactive in the behavioral responses, mental tapes, emotional defaults, and circumstantial outcomes in an individual's life narrative. When we align our choices with the authentic self, we feel strength through clarity and a dynamic flow that resonates with wholeness. When we do not align, we feel a sense of weakness, clouds of distortion that obscure our intention, and a divide with genuine integrity.

To seek the path of enlightenment is to seek empowerment in the will to co-create one's life narrative. This requires skill in the wielding of mindful awareness, a balance of responsibility, intentional manifestation, and surrender by actively witnessing the patterns of self, others, and the world. With this knowledge comes the opportunity to re-align and re-design the cyclical experiences and outcomes that feel confining, destructive, and unfulfilling, while magnifying the frequency of freedom, perpetual wholeness, and harmonic fulfillment. Becoming one with the authentic self may take many lives or events that challenge the mind, heart, and spirit to heal and lighten, beyond the weight of suffering. It may require the soul to face many paths of illusion that threaten to disconnect the nourishing origins and creative capacity of the authentic self. This causes pressure on one's integrity, the confidence to know truth, and to harness the power of intention within. Within darkness is the seed of light. Within light there is the seed of darkness. Both are integral to the balance of time and space, of birth and death, of life's losses and achievements. This interdependent relationship perpetuates possibility. It perpetuates what matters and what has yet to be understood as mattering. This possibility is constructed upon a cycle of sustainability, based in the essence of alchemical rebirth.

Alchemical living honors the existence of the authentic self and embarks upon the journey to discover it. Those that choose to align with their own authenticity and the universal authenticity share this integrity with the world, creating an invitation for others to align in their authentic self with shared transparency and accountability. This shared meeting of inherent value, in the experience of an individual, advocates respect and compassion when co-creating relationship and pursuing successful outcomes in life. Focusing effort and intention in the agreements we make with others and ourselves unlocks the expansive capacity for creative fulfillment in our endeavors, healing form perceived wounds, and untying karmic patterns that may dictate personal perceptions or the outcomes in our personal narrative. Through this effort we learn new ways to act with greater presence for what we align and create. Through practice these skills for transparency and presence become entrained and embodied, requiring less effort. The dance in the garden of life becomes lighter and brighter and the weight of the soul hovers on the scale of Anubis without fear or resistance to being seen.

- Deepen into the seeds of darkness and bring them to light. Acknowledge the strength within to align for healing beyond suffering. Choose transparency and discover the Authentic Self to create harmony within, releasing resistance to the journey of life. Dance on and be free, in the wings of your soul, for all to see. -

I

❦

Re-Establishing Root in Times of Change

When the pivotal tides of life have washed you upon new shores, how do you revive the light and the strength within to create again? How does the demand differ, based on the circumstances of the storm one perceives in their experience? Expanding the capacity for reserves that sustain the will required for persevering into new beginnings carries the same teaching, no matter how great the turbulence or graceful the drift. It is not the duration of time it is the perception of intensity and the dysregulation of coping mechanisms that drain one's being, disabling a sense of empowerment or purpose. Taking the time to restore and re-align with the Authentic self is an essential part of learning how to carry and protect the seeds of our dreams for cultivation in the future.

Nature moves in a dynamic cycle showing us the ways to bring creativity into production and fruition by nourishing the web of our roots after periods of harvest. The weather influences the shifts of the seasons as all creatures on the earth perceive different challenges to sustain necessities for success and attempt to cope with the extremes in excess or deficiency of resources. These patterns are directly relevant to how an individual perceives life events, demands for change, obstacles, loss, achievements, and self-sustainability mentally and emotionally. Finding a balance requires the awareness that balance is a perpetual dance in the everchanging landscape of life. An environment that moves in predictable and unpredictable ways nourishes the creative relationship of receptivity and action. Witnessing the pattern brings discernment of predictable and unpredictable factors, in order to find the empowering balance and grace when choosing the next steps to take.

The question is, are you a predictable or unpredictable factor in the experience? Centering within the wisdom of the Authentic self fortifies clarity for the foundational choices that define that self in every moment, regardless of situational variations. Without this cord of knowingness and self-trust, the more unpredictable one may be to themselves and any situation that arises. When an individual practices centering within the duality of life and mind with the receptivity to change, the clarity for how to dream forward will be refined and skillfully expanded through the unfolding seasons of life.

The power to create is nourished by the power to imagine. Humankind's ability to envision and manifest is the "Holy Grail" that perpetuates and evolves our experience as a species. How sacred we hold that grail and how willing we are to share it with others is one of the oldest questions recycled, again and again, throughout the tides of civilization in earth history. The power to dream is essential for perpetuating the value of one's experience in body on the earth or beyond what we know of this physical realm. The power to create is harnessed when the will to act on a dream is accessed, cultivated, and sustained. When life's demands and losses create forks in the road to a dream, the greatest opportunities arise to honor oneself and align accordingly with the deepest codes of personal truth. These codes are held deep in the web of our roots. The roots of our perceptions from childhood, repetitive life experiences, intuitive knowing, and awareness of the framework that defines who we are and who we choose to be in the give and take of life. Like a plant must conserve energy in times of drought or wait to release the buds of spring, one must focus their attention in the healing and tending to the roots of their own making. Without adequately nourished roots, a plants growth is stunted, diseased, or waning in the capacity for life, altogether.

Re-establishing roots in a changing world can seem daunting when every attempt to feel certainty for direction and success in manifestation continues to meet resistance. When a foundation is challenged for endurance in a time of renewal, the pace of attentive growth and healing to protect resources may become an all-consuming focus. Embracing the process of transformation and perspective for new ways to manage and succeed in the face of many knowns and unknowns is the most productive way to nourish curiosity while balancing self-protection and vulnerability. Learning the art of transformation secures and expands an individual's creative capacity within to become one with the divine flow that encourages refinement and re-design in perceptions of self as a part of the world. The magic of life is perpetuated by the mystery of the unknown and the cords of love that enlighten and empower us to imagine and then create. It is the inherent alchemical experience of transformation that shapes the heart, mind, and spirit for fulfillment, beyond suffering, that encodes the essence with joy in liberation and contentment in rooted connection.

Love is the nourishment for thriving. Love brings reconnection to self and connection to others. It is the healing salve for all wounds and the spark that perpetuates vitality. Love is demonstrated through one's sense of value and purpose. This must first be recognized by the self, for the self, and then by others, in mutual exchange, that share this loving recognition with one another. The seeds of our dreams revive dedication to focus our energy in times of renewal. Our perceptions of these seeded dreams are only fulfilling because of the love and gratitude discovered or sustained beyond the turmoil of change. Willpower alone is not enough to fulfill the holy grail within oneself. It may be enough to act with the integrity of the Authentic self, but it does not magnify or linger the way that the essence of love, as the foundation for value and purpose, feeds the soul. Feeding the soul is the only way to remembering how to dream. The spirit of love revives the will to cultivate the seeds of new beginnings. Trust in the Authentic self empowers the willing participation in the dance of life and embraces opportunity for the wisdom required to attain new degrees of fulfillment in the face of the unknown.

~ Catch your breath on the crystalline shores unfolding beneath you. Feel the light of the seeds in your pouch of dreams glowing with anticipation. Nourish your soul's truth in the web of your roots and embrace the essence of love and wisdom, strengthening each step to discover a new balance. Manifest by the will to thrive and radiate gratitude for existence. ~

II

◦◦◦

Weighing Trade-Offs
Through Choice

Trade-offs are the benefits and detriments we weigh, choose, and decline in every experience throughout life. The 1000-fold path many sages and yogis speak of is a stratum of possibility and probability created from the simplest choices we make in our day to day life. The mind tends to notice pivotal choices that affect larger scale structures in one's life journey, but even the smallest choices have their role to play in the symphony of one's personal narrative. Throughout the unfolding of experiences, an individual's personal narrative intersects and affects the narratives of others from the circumstances we are born into and later learn how to co-create. One's ability to problem-solve and assess the value of trade-offs is evident in the intentional effectiveness of their choices and corresponding outcomes.

Choices that lack intention and are based on impulse without prior reflection for outcomes and trade-offs tend to be less effective because they are less informed and therefore less calculated to achieve specified goals and desires. Once an individual learns at a young age, the power to have a choice, unintentional impulses and outcomes are still a form of choice. This choice tends to follow the path of trial and error, which perpetuates reasoning for lack of awareness and ambivalence around autonomy and accountability. The path of trial and error and the path of intention are both filled with many teachings. Trial and error approaches tend to feed narratives of martyrdom and victimhood, but the thrill of chance and surrender to cause and effect is its own language. Those that prefer higher levels of risk and rebel against the discipline required to unify heart and mind with clear intention tend to prefer this path. Likewise, those who seek to release themselves of the burdens of awareness that intentionality requires and feel the flow of fatalistic perceptions may also prefer this path.

The path of intention seeks to embody personal empowerment through sovereignty. Discerning trade-offs naturally promotes the process of differentiating wants from needs, as well as impulses and ideals from practical analysis and probabilities. Building consistent practices of analysis and expanding the multidimensional experience of the senses refines one's capacity to evaluate all forms of trade-offs. Trade-offs in choices made have the power to affect one mentally, emotionally, physically, and spiritually. These holistic aspects of being are interdependent factors in the patterns of experience that continually play out in our personal narratives. Understanding the value of trade-offs for oneself enables more creative problem solving for the purpose of accepting the greatest gains with lesser-valued losses. The path of trial and error and the path of intentional choice have their own trade-offs that may only be discerned by the individual choosing them for how it serves their narrative and preferred experiences in life.

Perceptions of what and how much an individual values something will always dictate one's draw to preserve it. When the focus of values is placed more on external sources, such as material things and people, there is less consideration in the quality of what one is gaining or giving up in their own sense of self. The awareness of personal values, integrity, and fulfilling deeper wants and needs in the authentic self may be minimized, compromised, or sacrificed repeatedly, when faced with the choices that request or require it. This happens more often when an individual values something or someone more than integrity with self. Weighing the effect of one's choices for gains and losses many times will affect others connected to the circumstances those trade-offs have unfolded in. Considering these affects as factors in the outcomes of one's choices is prudent if an individual values others. However, it is essential that the balance of compassion for self and compassion for others be honored in alignment with one's integrity to self when choices arise in shared circumstances and relationship. As more climactic events in life challenge an individual to evaluate trade-offs, primary wants and needs, and how to define and preserve their integrity with self and others, their capacity to make successful choices becomes evident.

Learning from the past to inform the present and align the future unfolding narrative is the most effective way to break through patterns of dissatisfaction and harm to discover the balance of co-creating with others and the forces of life. Practicing and witnessing the effects of change through choice in one's personal narrative supports the sustainability of trust and confidence with oneself as the journey continues. One of the most inspiring parts of life is that we have choice. We always have the choice to experience life events from different perspectives, to assess and refine our values, to learn new ways to achieve what nourishes the authentic soul or serves the ego, and the opportunity to choose again. One may not be able to change the past, specifically, but the trade-off for this is that an individual can witness it and evolve one's perceptions of trade-offs when choosing to walk the intentional or unintentional path in the future.

The interwoven existence of trade-offs will always bring the awareness of gains and losses. Perceptions of loss may create a sense of grief and resistance that burden the capacity for receptivity to the gains on the horizon. Time also affects an individual's experience of gains and losses, invoking patient anticipation or disregard, depending on the strain time casts over the circumstance. Continuing to reflect on personal values and perspectives as well as revealing blind spots in prior choices made, enables opportunities for discovering gains and losses one incurred without realizing. The simultaneous experience of grief and appreciation through relinquishing and being open to receive is a cornerstone in the alchemical process that empowers sentient embodiment in a physical world. Embracing awareness of self and being intentional in the choices an individual makes solidifies the alchemy that takes place in these moments. This potentiates the skills required to find enjoyment and peace for the outcomes of each trade-off. The acknowledgment for the alchemy of trade-offs advocates a journey toward sovereignty and fulfillment of the authentic self.

~ Open your hands to feel what is asking for release and what is coming to be received. Open your eyes deep within to evaluate intentions and values that honor the authentic self. Center your feet and feel the pivot that resonates with the wisdom of your own harmonic decree. ~

III

⚜

The Art of Anticipation, Patience, and Precision

"Time is of the essence.", some say. "Knowing is half the battle.", others say. "Make your mark.", another common phrase. These simple "roll off the tongue" phrases are reflections and ideals that may be interpreted in a variety of ways depending on the context in which they are used. The conscious interpretation may appear easily but the emotional layers of response change, revealing nuances in beliefs, values, and impulses that drive choices in the process to a desired outcome. Every path to a goal may be likened to our instinctual nature and learned skills like a hunter or gatherer seeking sustenance. The proverbial bow and arrow is a powerful symbol and practice for getting close to what one wants, managing the impulses of anticipation in order to focus on drawing the bow and releasing the arrow to the heart of its mark, at just the right time. This precision must be cultivated, not only left to chance. The skills for operating in unpredictable circumstances, no matter how familiar the terrain, are what expand one's chances for success.

Anticipation for our wants, fears, and curiosities is a primal behavioral response that becomes persistent alertness and leads to action, in most cases. Anticipating opens the door to many emotional responses prior to, during, and after the call to attention and action. Even if these emotional tides and conscious speculation are subdued into the subconscious for the purposes of staying focused and acting, they are there to be sorted, released, and resolved in order to act at all or to find contentment after taking action, in some way. When the emotional cords from more intense experiences go unresolved, they incite further anticipation for similar circumstances while keeping the mind and body connection from a sense of satisfaction or finality. When an individual does not acknowledge the behaviors that factored into an outcome, they decrease the opportunity to learn and practice effective behaviors as well as select out ineffective behaviors, misguided thoughts, and misdirected emotions. These un-witnessed or unattended elements are what most often lead to poor precision.

Finding the stillness within during the experience of anticipation helps one cultivate the skill of patience. In this stillness, the flow of awareness begins to allow broader implications of what is perceived in the environmental factors surrounding a goal or intention. It also fine-tunes an individual's focus on the best strategies that become apparent in the path to achieving a desired outcome. If the best strategies are not apparent, it gives an individual time and space to research new approaches, enlist the help of others, or clarify whether there is a need or desire to act, at all. Without the capacity to subdue anticipation and the call to action, an individual will struggle with the fall out of impulsive responses, overcompensations, and unseen factors that mire holistic perceptions of success. However, the experience of anticipation also exists as a catalyst in times of procrastination or ambivalence. It also reflects and augments enthusiasm for enjoyment and relief. This is important to remember for those that perceive anxiety, automatically, when a sense of anticipation occurs or cycles. Context will always clarify the role anticipation has to play when aligning intention and responses to circumstance.

Immediate responses can be successful and empowering when they are informed by previous patterns of cultivation in awareness of oneself, outside factors, the assessment of strategic choices, and what becomes a practiced form of precision through embodied wisdom and instinct. Impulsive responses may be immediate but they lack the process of full assessment, clarity of intention for outcomes, and well-informed behaviors for precision. Finding stillness in the eye of cyclical anticipation engages the wisdom of patience and total embodiment of a choice that may be executed at any pace one finds necessary with the holistic control of the mental, physical, and emotional body. Teachings of the Japanese Samurai and the book of "Bushido" are an excellent reference for considering the real and metaphorical value of strategy, centering oneself, and successfully resolving challenges in life. The same concerns for fighting challenges and adversaries outside ourselves must be mutually applied to the internal conflicts and barriers that arise within oneself.

The journey of life is a collection of many journeys within it. Remembering that a journey is a process with short-term and long-term effects, dictated by the trade-offs of one's choices, is essential when the experience of anticipation arises and when it begins to feel persistent. You are the bow and your choices are the arrows. Clarity of vision, the balance of emotional tension and flow, confidence in the assessment of known and unknown factors, and the wisdom of direct or vicarious experiences are the power that leads the relationship of the bow and arrow as a unified force. The bend, the notches, the grains, the give and the resistance are all integrated into the artistry of the bow, itself. Your inherent qualities and learned behaviors as well as your dedication to practicing and forming connection with your abilities and desires for achievement are all apparent in the arc of your arrows to their intended or unintended mark, defined by successes, near misses, and lost opportunities.

The art of anticipation, patience, and precision can be a fun and intriguing process. It requires the curiosity to discover, the discipline for efficiency, and the focus to develop strength for an invaluable life skill. It also requires surrender to what an individual cannot see or does not know yet, along with compassion for self when the bow resists or the arrow misses its mark. A successful archer must get in closer to their intended goal, understand the nuances of nature, and the effect of oneself on the environment for proper alignment and timing. Embracing the many layers of self through mindful awareness and radical accountability will unlock the evolving experience of effortlessness, even though focused effort will always be required. This sense of focused effort is necessary to act or to yield in the circumstances surrounding a desired goal. The effortlessness is a sensation that arises with familiarity to one's abilities, confidence in the accuracy of one's choices, and the caliber of successes through lived experience. A steady hand and an acute eye will show precision many times more than an emotionally charged impulse and blurred understandings of purpose toward a valued outcome.

Every archer must make the time and effort to learn how they operate in familiar and unknown circumstances. When gathering or hunting, it is essential to observe and learn new environments or how familiar places have changed with the seasons. The landscape of belief, emotional awareness, and an individual's aptitude for connection to the intrinsic resonance of an endeavor are keys to understanding what is required to align and achieve intended fulfillment. The balance of perspective between a broader view of the land and the details layered within it that pose variables to navigate through to a goal is paramount for precision before one acts. This metaphor for perception applies to the external world as well as the terrain within oneself.

If an individual tends to see the details, one must remember to step back, see the big picture, and weigh perceptions of value in the relationships of those details when filtering fixations and discerning meaning. If an individual tends to see the big picture, one must remember to deepen into the network of intrinsic elements to define the bias of one's overview before dismissing the inherent value of those elements. Choosing one mode of perspective sets the heart and mind up to be snared by illusion and folly. Finding a balance between one's bottom-line perception and attachment to experiential details is essential to aligning with a well-informed truth as well as the choice to identify with that truth. Clarity and confidence in one's truth aligns the arrow for precision. With the balanced anticipation of an open heart and the patience of a steady hand, the bow will bend with resilience through the journey to achieve finality and fulfillment in every season of life.

- As the wind builds and the landscape moves, find your center, and go within. Feel the rhythm of life's tides swelling with anticipation and let your roots grow deep beneath the current until you sense solid ground to steady perspective. Harken your ear to the song of clarified intention and draw your bow with the wisdom of patience. Pivot and align in time, releasing the arrow, in the exhale of appreciation and creative inspiration. -

IV

֍

The Logos of Interdependent Relationship

Relationships come in all flavors of intentional or unintentional agreement that may involve behaviors of independence, co-dependence, or interdependence. The fulfillment and security within a relationship requires acknowledgment of what we have agreed to by learning the other through shared experience and the roles each naturally default into. The hunt for fulfillment and security in connection also includes the continued agreements for what each person values, what they want to continue sharing, and what they intend to create with one another. A relationship between two people may ask many things of each individual throughout the course of relating, building, maintaining, and healing a bond. If both individuals value the connection equally and carry the intention to nurture a sense of loyalty, trust, and deeper understanding of one another, the bond thrives. When there is a perceived imbalance in the exchange that creates conflict, each individual's devotion to harmony within the relationship is called upon to show effort and find mutual understanding that strengthens their devotion and sense of unity in connection. Throughout the maturation process of relationship cohesion, power struggles for autonomy, and desire for acts of devotion will arise to challenge and refine every individual's way of sharing and co-creating that simultaneously honors the authentic self and the soul of relationship. The closer we each become to defining our own authenticity, the more important the balance in our relationship agreements becomes apparent.

The logos of interdependent relationship looms in the heart of the authentic self, calling for healthy boundaries, agreements for exchange, and a sense of fulfilled acknowledgment for the gifts we all have to share that enable connection with other. Reaching interdependence requires clarity of mind, acknowledgment of the heart's emotions, and witnessing the soul of relationship that inspires both individuals into co-creating devotion with one another. This is relevant to friends, family, lover, and partner relationships. It may also be found in business relationships with more or less emotional involvement, depending on the individuals and their accepted roles within a professional framework. Interdependence is exhibited and achieved by mindful awareness of self, other, and the relationship. Through mutual consideration of self, other, intentional agreements, and the soulful essence of the relationship, the path to unity is easier to maintain. Attentiveness to the misperceptions, confusion, feelings of separation, or refinement of values, may be resolved quicker through the use of compassionate communication that honors both individuals.

When both individuals bring their authentic self to create

connection, it is essential to find compromise and alignment that supports the integrity of both individuals and does not break down into reactive judgments, emotional manipulation, or struggles for power that negate win-win opportunities through effective problem solving. If agreement cannot be found that honors the authentic self of both individuals then stalemate may conclude departure from previously agreed upon roles or expectations to co-create further with one another, at all. The hallmark ending of interdependent relationship beyond the initial grieving responses is distinguished through mutual gratitude and sense of elevation both individuals feel for the experiential memories co-created and expanded upon for fulfillment within their exchange. It is never easy to let go of those we love and have felt greatly fulfilled by, yet the love and acknowledgment from honoring each other perpetuates beyond the strife of separation in life or death. This is the way of humility through grief and integrity with gratitude for the gifts we have shared.

Throughout the journey of building and refining connection, co-dependency or strong independence tend to be more common. As children, we are born into the experience of co-dependency with our mother and possibly with other parental figures or siblings. Forced independence at a young developmental stage can shift attitudes of expectation in future connections, depending on one's response to feelings of abandonment and helplessness or resilience and resourcefulness. Likewise, the experience of smothering, sheltering, and always getting what we want when we ask for or demand it without the opportunity to compromise and take self-responsibility, will also create unproductive behaviors that affect relationship dynamics and outcomes. Many times, all of these experiences around expectation are interwoven, enabling more or less productive coping mechanisms that dictate types of attachment and detachment behavior. Until acknowledged, reviewed, and harmonized through the experience of connection and one's self-discovery, these behaviors can create conflict with others and a lack of fulfillment in relationship.

Co-dependent relationships are primarily founded in a sacrifice of the authentic self, by one or both individuals. Conflicts and disagreements often end in win-lose resolution or emotional dominance and submission dynamics that parade the illusion of devotion through martyrdom or victimization. This devotion comes at a high cost and is often very fragile. Both individuals tend toward dissatisfaction easily because the desire to be acknowledged and honored for their authentic self is stronger deep within. This causes a perpetual struggle for autonomy or a loss of self through consignment of personal will to another. The authentic self wants to be seen and heard. Its gravity beneath the surface will continue to push upward and create opportunities for an individual to discover, heal, and consciously unify with these essential pieces of their identity. Co-dependent relationship patterns can be witnessed as opportunities to grow and learn more about what is calling for healing in the mind and heart. These experiential narratives can unveil a path to writing a new story that challenges the application of one's newfound values and creative focus toward defining more fulfilling connection in personal relationships.

Some relationships are marked by mutual independence, where both individuals enjoy time together but are focused on self and their own path without needing to share responsibility or weigh out choices with concern for how the other in relationship will be affected. These relationships are most often friendships, but may also occur in lover, partner, or adult family relationships. When mutual independence is the framework of connection, the ease of disregard, removal, and dissolution of the bond can arise more quickly in moments of disagreement. This approach to relationship creates opportunities to co-exist and appreciate others without the intensity and depth of devotion or mutual dedication to grow through the pressures that closer and more attentive bonds bring. While there may be honest appreciation, respect, and fulfilling exchanges in a mutually independent relationship, the investment for sustainability, the efforts for compassionate resolutions, and the discovery of intimacy through sharing and revealing the authentic self are less likely to occur. Discovering a sense of independence, beyond co-dependence, in oneself with the intention for healthy self-reliance is another layer of maturation in the heart and mind on the path to creating fulfilling connection with self and others. Discovering one's capacity for self-reliance and appreciation for directing one's life experiences without the need for others to govern, placate, or provide these choices and opportunities is foundational to discerning what interdependent relationship may look and feel like, in alignment with one's authentic self.

Interdependent relationships are distinguished by their capacity to perpetuate opportunities for creating, growing, sharing, and witnessing our loved ones heal throughout life into their truest self. Compassion, problem solving, acknowledging trade-offs in choices, and devotion with healthy boundaries are all essential components of meeting another on common ground. These components support intentions of mutual dedication and attentiveness for unity in connection beyond conflicts and misunderstanding in the perceptions of each other. The dance of interdependence includes practicing discernment instead of judgment, releasing the need to control an outcome for personal gain that negates win-win solutions that both individuals value, and resolving power struggles for autonomy through the awareness and refinement of intentional agreements. Intentional agreements secure the heart and soul of relationship.

They create a framework for the mind when irrationality or over-rationalizing arise as a response to the circumstances of life. One's sense of loyalty and integrity with self and others will always influence the types of relationship they create and their ultimate outcomes. The logos of interdependence is a seed planted deep in the soul. It is born into experience and thrives within every compulsion for connection. Seeking and honoring the authentic self forges the doorway that opens a path to mutually empowering relationships with others that reflect the heart-centered values of sustainable bonds founded in the blossoming logos of interdependence.

~ Embrace your inner child with love and curiosity. Listen deep to the balance of serving self and other. Choose power over no one but thyself and behold gratitude for the gifts exchanged. Expand awareness for the call of soul that speaks in the foundations of every relationship. ~

V

⸨✥⸩

Paths to Intimacy through Authenticity

The path to intimacy is a journey in learning, understanding, and sharing experiences with another through embracing the deeper value of connection with self and each other. Intimacy is most often created in our closest and longest relationships. This includes family, friends, and romantic partners. It is not about sexual union, although preceding associations in religion and society have simplified it to this. Truly intimate relationships are founded in mutual transparency and mutual respect with another. Honesty and deeper connection with the authentic self is a prerequisite to establish true intimacy with others. These foundational elements create a sustainable invitation to witness one another and share devotion in support of growth for each individual through life experiences. The perpetuation of confidence, curiosity, effort for creative problem solving in times of distress, and loyalty to shared values are all interdependent elements for the evolution of trust in order to strengthen the bonds of intimacy.

When one or more of these elements are lost, a sense of separation and loss of intimacy is felt to some degree. Distinguishing what feels compromised or lost in a connection when this occurs is essential to refining communication for both individuals. Intimacy is a braided cord woven through the act of witnessing, discernment, compassionate communication, clarity of values, shared codes of loyalty, and defined expectations. Many other fibers of one's being are threaded into the cords of intimacy. The present, nostalgic, or future imagery an individual carries about self or with other affects the tension and resistance in this braided cord. This is why discovering the authentic self through mindful awareness in patterns of behavior, thought, desire, and resistance is not only foundational, but integral to the successive experience of intimacy.

Authenticity is an experience we perpetuate and learn to embody once freed from resistance to vulnerability. The pearls of introspection and reflection on the experiences of and with others, grants an individual greater opportunities to manifest more fulfilling outcomes in life. These outcomes strengthen perceptions of healthy continuity when witnessing self and relationships with others. Choosing vulnerability with an open heart opens the door to empowering more meaningful, enduring, and co-creative connection, while balanced practices of interdependence safeguard the will of the authentic self. Intimacy increases a sense of security and strength in the bonds we hold sacred. Knowing and sharing one's true self is the beginning of the path to intimacy with oneself as well as with another. If we cannot be transparent and intimate with ourselves through introspection, we cannot offer this to others.

Intimacy is an experience most, if not all, humans crave. Even if resistance to life, denial of self, and abstaining from inter-relational moments with others has become the norm for someone taught this behavior or reacting to the hardships of life, the authentic self within still craves to be seen and valued. Choosing the long walk of healing and re-learning ways of being will begin to reveal this calling for connection, appreciation of understanding, and value in mutual confidence. Choosing intimacy means choosing vulnerability to the loss of intimacy and the cathartic emotions of the grieving process that come with that loss.

Once intimacy is created, the goal is to sustain the experience and trust of that intimacy as sacred with self and with others. Even if the degrees of intimacy change form throughout the journey to define and refine the authentic self on an individual's personal journey or between both individuals in a relationship, the appreciation and intention to remain steadfast in the effort to re-create devotion to self or with another in relationship must be retained in order to return to a deepened sense of intimacy through self-knowing, self-value, and sharing that self with others. When all sense of intimacy feels lost with another, it is important to honor the value of what was shared, even if it is no longer in alignment with one's present journey. Through continued acknowledgement, the sacred potency of that lost intimacy may continue to serve the authentic self in the next stages of growth and deeper understanding of the path we all share as sentient beings in human form.

Would you have rather foregone the experience than receive this gift? There are trade-offs in every moment one chooses to create. Can you assess the trade-offs of your choices and what has been learned to refine your choices and trade-offs as you move forward? Holding onto the illumination empowers greater degrees of honesty and intimacy with self and others as every individual learns how to manifest and effectively co-create fulfillment in the experience of life. The path to intimacy is how we deepen our reflection of self through the eyes of others and discern a core sense of knowing that withstands superficial judgments, misperceptions, and the weathering of life events. Choosing intimacy is an active embrace of the alchemical transformation inherent in relationship with humans and the forces of nature.

~ Unfold the sacred petals of your soul through the light of the heart and sustain the effort to perpetuate compassionate interdependence. Create invitation for discovery, healing, and evolution to succeed on the path of intimacy. ~

VI

~~~

Evaluating Exchange and Discerning Give and Take

Every relationship we enter is founded in the experience of exchange. Witnessing and discerning what feels fulfilling about the exchange is essential for the perpetuation of that exchange. In many scenarios, exchange may be objectively perceived as imbalanced due to the roles each person takes on. This does not mean the exchange is unfulfilling if those within it prefer to have an imbalance of power in what is given and what is taken, as a trade-off for what each person values most. This imbalance of power most often perpetuates in co-dependent relationships or for individuals lacking self-direction and self-reliance that seek independent and ambitious individuals to support them mentally, emotionally, physically, and/or financially. As emotions shift in life circumstances the subjective experience of exchange can be confusing, misinterpreted, or strained by demand. The stereotypical "givers and takers" exist but there are very clear ways in which they behave. The perceived balance of exchange in any relationship will be challenged as life circumstances request different kinds of support from both individuals. Every individual wants to feel value in what they bring to relationship and what they receive from it.

The search for mutuality and a balance of power in relationship is discerned through the behaviors of reciprocation, communication, and accountability with agreements. Truly honoring an exchange is founded in the acknowledgment for what one is giving and receiving. Communicating the appreciation for this is confirmation of value in what each person has to offer. One should only give what they want to give as well as being honest with themselves and others when it comes to expectations or needs in return. This clarifies and reduces the frequency of misperception and disillusionment that can occur in the capricious applications of perception around give and take, which are affected by the fluidity of emotions that arise in differing life circumstances.

The act of giving is inherently a fulfilling experience for the heart and mind. Most individuals feel gratification when they give to others and see or feel appreciation in return. It is an automatic feeling of being accepted, acknowledged, and valued for the person perceiving what they have given when it is received by another. Yet, the person receiving may value the offering more or less then the person giving it and although there is no definitive way to influence the value of what was given to the receiver, clearly stated intentions or requests by the giver about what has been given can open a path to understanding the value of the exchange for both individuals. Many people who enjoy giving will say they do not require anything in return, even if they do want or require the most basic acknowledgment and appreciation vocally from the receiver or via reciprocation at another time in the relationship. Does true altruism exist? This question has been an ongoing discussion in the realm of psychology. Everyone benefits and receives esteem from being valued for who they perceive themselves to be and what they perceive they give to others.

How capable are you of giving without receiving acknowledgment or the confirmation from others of who you are by what you give? Are you capable of still giving to others and only being the one to acknowledge and feel confirmation of who you are to yourself? This skill is necessary in times of confusion, disregard, and feeling devalued by others. To utilize it effectively requires a sense of accountability and worthiness, integrated by compassion for self and others through objectivity, in order to accurately review the present conflict about an exchange and the historical evidence of exchange founded in the relationship roles and agreements. If valuing oneself has become the only focus in a moment that one feels a lack of appreciation or reciprocation, self-entitlement may lead to self-sabotage, especially if the other individual is not truly a "taker" stereotype and misperceptions are ruling one's ego to safeguard worthiness.

The give and take between self and others are a part of bonding through service to each other and to the relationship. A healthy exchange that is tended to frequently, through devotion to the bond shared, enables the possibility of interdependent relationship. Clarity and accountability for the agreements we make and roles we take on in relationship is essential for founding and evolving that relationship out of separateness from independent attitudes or power conflicts that arise from co-dependent behaviors. True devotion is not co-dependency. Devotion requires active choosing to give and share with another and gratitude for those moments is the hallmark of devotions' offering for all involved. Healthy devotion from an open heart for self and other has the power to heal, uplift, and continually return us to the light of our authentic self. Devotion to self and devotion to other is a choice we make every day. Devotion is continually created between those who seek to honor and acknowledge one another with gratitude, no matter the confusion, hardship, and conflicts that unfold in human perception when pursuing understanding and navigating what we agree to. Seeking the values of interdependence when creating and discerning exchange in relationships engages deeper layers of fulfillment in an individual and society, collectively.

The stereotypes of "giver" and "taker" become more valid and applicable during times of destabilization in an individual's life and in societal constructs. This is when the basic drives for survival and clinging to what one fears will be scarce or has already been lost consume perceptions of an experience. The formative elements of a personality are brought forth in the highest periods of stress endured in an individual's life or a community experiencing disaster. Some come together to help others and help each other, while others isolate and refuse to take part with a focus on helping themselves. Throughout life, people may move back and forth between the identities of giver and taker. However, some will find it hard to admit they are a taker if they are in fact, only a taker. Most good-natured people that seek healthy exchange will admit when they feel they have been more on the receiving end. These same people will often attempt to reciprocate, so they feel good about receiving. It is important that the giver be open to receiving and allow these opportunities for reciprocation to nurture a bond of interdependence.

When weighing the balance of give and take in relationship, one's foundational perspective of themselves in life will dictate what they can or will acknowledge for what they and others have given. People who feel like they never have enough or that the "anonymous they" in the world owe them will always focus more on what they are giving and what others are taking. It is common to disregard what they are receiving in exchange from others when they are only focused on the void within that feels unquenchable. People who feel like they are always giving without receiving much in return may be unable to see how they have not placed proper boundary with self when feeling compelled to give, especially if they have an alternate agenda for expectations to be met as a part of an exchange that have not been communicated. People who tend to give a lot and feel an imbalance in return must ask themselves if they are truly open to receiving, as well as capable of asking for what they need or want to feel a balanced exchange. They must also reflect on whether they value what another has to offer in exchange to reach fulfillment. Then, they must create opportunities for that fulfillment to occur. True "taker" stereotypes take what they can with minimal acknowledgment for those sharing with them and will not openly offer anything in exchange. True takers express or exhibit entitled statements and attitudes. The "giver" stereotype gives without concern for what they are getting in return. They may be the self-sacrificial doormats of relationship and society or they may be the unconditionally loving sage that trusts what they give is in service to the highest good. They may feel undeserving of gifts or they may have resilience in their cycle of self-appreciation and esteem by valuing themselves through what they see their gifts produce for another or society. Most people enter relationship conditionally and have wants and needs they bring to the exchange. There are many ways to give and to receive that are valuable in the exchange of relationship for shared fulfillment in the outcomes of life experiences. When life changes, the balance of give and take in relationships may change as well. It is up to all involved to pursue clarity for conflicts that occur around give and take in relationship. If the goal is to sustain a sense of value for that relationship this may be accomplished through compassionate communication, accountability, and refined agreements.

~ Step into the center of yourself when a sense of lack arises. Acknowledge the values you hold most dear and the experience of gratitude for self and other that founded the bond and desire for exchange. Be honest in what you have to give and want to receive. Seek creative solutions that bring healing through closure or opportunities for renewed devotion. ~

VII

⚜

Offerings and Invitations

What would it be like to perceive and direct experiences in life from a place of offerings and invitations? How would it feel to embrace every shared communication as an opportunity to witness different perspectives and to cultivate skill in the use of intentional choice? The weblike journey through our relationships to self and others, as well as an individual's orientation to the experience of living, casts out and catches a plethora of requirements and demands mixed with offerings and invitations. In a world that focuses on power struggles and the drama of conflict for survival, a feedback system for the reality we create is perpetuated in the consciousness of self and the collective. This feedback system thrives by the perceptions we carry within that orient our behaviors when moments of change and choice arise. Conflicts with self and others are the fertile moments that set the sails, based on the navigation of one's receptivity to personal growth and co-creating with others. Conflicts present opportunities to refine perspectives with new information and to step out of the storm of power struggles. This is achieved by becoming an objective witness of the experience, in order to acknowledge the trade-offs of offerings and invitations with requirements and demands.

Offerings may arise as direct favors and physical gifts, but they are also the simple or profound moments of shared observation, analysis, and advice that are in service to personal desires and resolving conflicts. The latter form of offerings, often invoke a question or weighing out of ideals, thoughts, and/or feelings about a specific subject or occurrence in one's life. These offerings may originate from within an individual's mental processing or "self-talk" and from others that are delivered intentionally in a compassionate, guiding way. If the one receiving the offering perceives judgments or assumptions are being made by another, this is an indication that the communication was not neutral in its delivery or that one is unable to receive due to their own overlay of self-judgment, assumption, and defensiveness. This type of perception may be a prevalent pattern in how they interact with others or perceive any observation made or spoken of them.

Bias is an inherent part of consciousness within self. Any event, concept, or feeling is tied to the individual perceiving, analyzing, and responding to it. Bias creates resistance to empathy and consideration for the thoughts and feelings of others, which shuts down the flow of receptivity in communication and connection. Bias can mire one's vision like looking through dirt-coated glasses. You always see the dirt first, even if it has become so normalized that you ignore it's on your lens, and it takes effort to truly see beyond it without cleaning the lens of perspective. When one is unaware of their own biases or does not take the time to re-assess them, receptivity to other points of view and the commonality of "judgmental listening" resists a path to healthy communication with self and others. It is unlikely that bias will ever be fully removed from the individual or the moment that one is seeking resolve and confidence with, but with awareness and effort all of us have the opportunity to acknowledge our bias and clear, subdue, or substantiate and uphold the bias we decide is most important. By clearing distorted, inapplicable, or unsubstantiated bias and lesser valued biases, one can be open to more fulfilling solutions while simultaneously resolving much of the emotional reactivity and internal or external conflict that arises in the defense or demand of bias. This allows a clarified and centered focus on what matters most. It also consolidates the energy needed to achieve it within self or in discourse with others.

If an offering is perceived as an insult or overreach, it is the responsibility of the individual who feels that way to communicate their perception or confusion about it for maintaining rapport or to take the time to discern what it means beyond the initial experience of it on their own. It is important to understand that when misperception without honorable transparency and the disregard for clarity occurs, the original offering no matter how loving and considerate may be used as a mast to standby in self-righteousness or one to cut away by an unyielding mind. For the giver, it is key to remember that the altruistic offering does not require a return like an invitation. It may not even require acknowledgment, although this is the most considerate form of discourse. It is a gift without attachment to how it is valued. In the current climate of social exchange it is common for offerings to be missed, disregarded, inaccurately perceived, and judged in the projections of others struggling to sustain an open heart and mind with less confounding bias. Having confidence in self for the offerings given with integrity and consideration of others is all that is required by the self if it is truly an offering.

An invitation is an offering that carries expectation for response or action. When someone puts forth an invitation, the origin comes from an open heart and mind that seeks the opportunity to share something with another. What is shared may be a moment, advice, or an object that is dividable or transferable. The moment or advice proposed by an invitation may carry any number of possibilities with respect to purpose and who it serves. It may serve the "inviter" initially, but also carry positive returns for the "invitee". It may predominantly serve the "invitee" if accepted and acted upon, or it may serve others beyond the "inviter" and "invitee". Ultimately, all true invitations carry the opportunity for everyone to benefit in some way, even if this benefit is not equally weighted. The difference between offerings and invitations is the attachment to an exchange that is about intentional sharing. Altruism is not inherent in an invitation as it is with an offering due to an individual's expectation for the obligation of response that accepts or denies the invitation directly. Offerings and invitations are similar in their root of open-minded and open-hearted intention to put forth possibility without the requirement or demand of acting upon it that create definable consequences for self and others. However, the effort and intention to communicate effectively and authentically to achieve receptivity with self and others, is essential to clearly distinguish offerings and invitations from requests and demands.

When consequences are put forth in a negotiation with self or others, the feelings that arise may evolve through the analysis of those consequences. Often, the root of these feelings is initiated by surprise, fear, or anger about having to choose consequences at all or with the limitation of the specific consequences that are defined. The building pressure in the psyche for liberation and fulfillment or closure and resolve can skew one's impressions of the moment presenting as demands or requests. Until the emotional experience is subdued and the objective role of the witness in self takes over the perception of demand versus request, the clarity for how to weigh consequences of choice will be obscured.

Requests are similar to invitations, yet requests carry a specific need to be fulfilled. If the need is not fulfilled, regardless of the individual's perception of the request directed at them, a clear consequence of inaction, poor action, or opposing action will be stated or revealed. Sensing defined or undefined consequences is an instinct most individuals carry within. The tone, delivery, and placement of requests are often distinguished by circumstance. The circumstantial experience may involve direct conflict or nuances of constructive observation leading to requirement. With respect to personal and interpersonal relationships, demands may present in the form of authoritative assertions that evolve out of requests. This occurs when an individual believes that what is needed must be fulfilled by the person that they are demanding it from. Demands often carry larger consequences than requests due to the perceived infringement of emotion and severity of obligation for fulfillment, which is evident in backlash behaviors. Although demands may also be slightly intensified requests without backlash behavior, they are clearly defined by the assertion that an imbalance of power exists, either within self or with others in relationship to self. Beware that the emotional intensity often displayed within a demand or felt by a demand can parade the illusion of power being taken or lost, but free will to respond in a way that seeks to harmonize a perceived power struggle in communication is always there. It is the responsibility of those involved to weigh responsibility and reflect on the power of demands as well as the choices available for mutual fulfillment or mutual resolve. It is also the responsibility of every individual to themselves to assess what they are willing to agree to as well as their ability to follow through on that agreement. When mutual fulfillment and a balance of power has met a stalemate, it is natural and most beneficial for every individual to remain empowered and reconsider paths to self-reliance and self-resolve.

The ideals of harmonization, negotiation, and mutual consideration are founded in compassionate communication and compersion that are focused through the intentional practice of offerings and invitations. Managing awareness of the authentic self and attending to one's needs for fulfillment within, before seeking offerings and exchanges with external sources, is the most effective approach to achieving perceived harmony. In relationship to self and others it is inevitable for requests to form and evolve as well as the assessment of trade-offs in consequences to be cultivated. If one maintains awareness in what fulfills the authentic self while managing healthy boundaries, adaptability, and objectivity for perceived choices and outcomes when wants or needs for self or others arise, the occurrence of demands from self to others will be less. Likewise, the emotional response to the demands of others to self will feel less overpowering. This allows a balance of power to be negotiated through requests or equally demanded for fulfillment and resolve.

Engaging with life through the intentional act of witnessing self and others enables the opportunity for intentional communication, in order to achieve the most harmonic outcomes for all. Seeking harmonic fulfillment and a balance of power in one's internal dialogue and exchanges with others cultivates sustainable and healthy relationships that mutually serve the intelligence of those involved. The approach of invitations, offerings, and requests honors free will and upholds the integrity of the authentic self. True respect is only found where the integrity of oneself is evident in their words and actions, which requires a balance of power and responsibility. Leading with an open heart and mind is essential to compassionate communication, adaptability for negotiation, confidence with establishing boundaries, and clarity for the effort put forth to achieve receptivity.

~ Let offerings become a ritual of the heart and mind. Define the wants and needs within to discern the weight of invitations or requests, while cultivating reliance within. Balance the power of demands and align with what serves the authentic self to create harmony beyond resistance. ~

VIII

❧

Accountability is More than an Apology

Accountability is more than an apology. It is an honest communication that shows reflection, consideration, and discernment of one's actions that cause conflict. Accountability does not always require apology. If acknowledging one's choices, statements, and actions leads to understanding oneself better, how to improve, or how to resolve some perceived injustice, resolution can be met. Through accountability one can perpetuate agreements with self and connections with others that serve more fulfilling outcomes in the journey of the personal narrative we create.

Since childhood, we have been taught to apologize as a sign of acknowledgment and respect that we did something wrong. Sometimes those lessons came without explanation by the accuser or offended. Other times, the demand to elaborate and clarify what one did inaccurately or offensively was required for satisfying and resolving conflict. How often was the opportunity to problem solve or a distinguished plan of better action offered by the offender? How often did you make the effort to conclude and share your own discernment for how not to repeat perceived mistakes?

Apologies can be meaningful and apologies can just be hollow lip service. Apologies can be a way to deflect an issue or be used to feel accepted and continually valued in some way. Forgiveness can be fickle and resentment may still lurk beneath the surface if full accountability is not considered or offered. Likewise, opportunities to apply creative solutions to change behaviors in order to resolve repetitive conflict, is necessary to build trust and support stated expectations that are agreed upon. There are many times words and actions are not in alignment. This is natural in the learning phase if an individual seeks growth. Compassion for the process and objective discernment are essential in assessing one's capacity to be accountable and align their intentions with evident behaviors over time. This means it is important to recognize when some individuals are unable to track their own behaviors due to lack of development in self-awareness. Compassionate communication is a helpful tool to utilize when navigating experiences with them that feel redundant or frustrating. If progress is fleeting, one must decide to accept the individual as they are or distance themselves from the connection beyond the direct effects of their behaviors.

The applications of understanding and stated intentions to act differently are the evidence that accountability is being preserved or created anew. An individual's behaviors, whether intentional or impulsive, are the leading communication to self and others for the value placed on meaningful exchange. Words are powerful and carry the nuances of emotion that present for persuasion, inspiration, and comfort, as well as disregard, disapproval, or rejection. "Actions speak louder than words" is an age-old saying because in our minds and our hearts we are drawn to believe what we are hearing more than what we are seeing. This creates disillusionment and dissatisfaction that leads to divisiveness in one's perceptions of themselves or others. When it is more ephemeral, as "words on the wind", the bastions of hope and doubt lead the convictions of perception. When ephemeral words become rooted as embodied behaviors, the holistic messaging of words and behaviors dissolves the persistence of hope and doubt. A clear pattern of expectation, whether new or pre-existing, then has a foundation to build upon for experiential awareness and fulfillment within self and in relationship with others.

It is common in relationships with others and the relationship with oneself, "to brush things under the rug" for the sake of being ok or happy in the moment. This deferral response is a defense mechanism designed to keep one from feeling the conflict of guilt, resentment, regret, or other informative emotions. While defense mechanisms can be helpful to keep an individual focused on what matters most, letting them become a repetitive way to defer conflict and the deeper meaning of those provocative stimuli negates connection to the authentic self and the integrity of relationship with other. Choosing to acknowledge the source of these provocations and defense mechanisms brings an individual closer to accountability, to what is of value, and what may be calling for healing in self or the soul of relationship with other. Choosing accountability over deferral is a noble act that can diffuse and equalize power struggles within self and in relationship. By doing so, an individual acknowledges personal behaviors and traits they choose to stand by in the wisdom of honoring self and when applicable, a path to refining them for better outcomes.

The perceptions of right and wrong, honoring one's personal truth, and emotional experience will always be subjective to the individual. They will also be relative to the context of a situation and agreements made with self or others. We are all fine-tuning a compass within to meet the invitations of our most authentic self. Accountability with the agreements we make with ourselves and those we make with others is essential to strengthen the embodied potency of our most authentic self. Honorable transparency with one's sorted and concluded thoughts or stated confusion with mixed emotions is equally important when accepting accountability for one's role in any circumstance. Beyond acceptance, comes the opportunity for healing and problem solving, alone or with others. Sharing creative solutions with others that may be involved in current circumstances with intentional offering or invitation supports mutual resolve and appreciation for how to honor an agreement or modify it, in order to move forward.

Accountability is the cultivation of honoring one's truth and perceived role in all situations, including the way an individual chooses to acknowledge their abilities to act or not act, to react, or to respond to an experience or another person in shared experiences. Accountability is not only applicable to conflicts, apologies, and problem solving. It is in direct relationship to the acknowledgment of one's choices and actions that affect outcomes in celebratory or positive circumstances, as well. The difference between acknowledgment and accountability is that acknowledgment is passive and reflective, while accountability is active and productive. Acknowledgment provides a path for accountability to be applied. Both bring healing to the soul and to relationship with others. They are each required to weave a deeper sense of knowing, trust, and intimacy with the authentic self as well as relationships with others.

Radical self-acceptance is not the same as radical accountability. The difference between acceptance and accountability is the investment in one's choices, how they affect outcomes, and the impetus to deepen responsibility for personal patterns of behavior that an individual perceives, either as justifiable or in need of justification. This process upholds integrity with self and others. Self-acceptance does not require awareness of how an individual effects outcomes, nor does it require further motivation to justify patterns of behavior and the health of one's choices. The capacity for accountability is an essential attribute for assessment of an individual's integrity with themselves and others.

~ Open your heart and mind to tune the compass within. Seek honorable transparency when weighing and choosing the value of acceptance and accountability to grow beyond what you know of yourself. Embody intention to manifest behaviors that align with the integrity of your authentic self and experience the definition of wholeness. ~

IX

❧❧❧

Choosing Love as a Legacy

The paths we take in life are initiated by fate and free will. The emotional experiences one perceives affect one's sense of completion or lack of resolve. Finding fulfillment or reaching closure in each experience enhances a sense of contentment that inspires us to move forward with empowered curiosity through the changes each path presents. Experiences that result in a lack of resolve may spur one forward onto new journeys as well, yet the quality of this emotional void calling for fulfillment and closure requires many coping mechanisms to be learned or employed. As life unfolds, considerations about one's personal narrative arise in alignment with events that define new stages of growth and accomplishment or disillusion and loss. The wake of satisfaction or unresolve one sees reflected in their path invokes thoughts and feelings about the legacy they are imprinting on the world and those they share it with. Choosing to share a legacy of love is the greatest gift one can give to others and to oneself.

The mantras we carry every day in our heart and mind dictate many aspects of what we create and how we perceive opportunities for resolve or fulfillment. Mantras in the mind are repetitive loops and phrases one tells themselves. These mantras may be provoked as a natural response to an experience or invoked as an affirmative choice within that experience. Mantras may create positive or negative reinforcement about one's perceptions of self, others, and life circumstance. Acknowledging the mental loops that occur when processing an experience allows one to question the deeper implications and evidence for where those thoughts come from or how they do and do not serve outcomes for self-resolve or fulfillment. We each have the power to master the feeling of authentic resonance with affirmations that are founded in compassionate strength to endure and create greater opportunities in learning how to problem-solve. This ability empowers many skills for life success. It is essential to choose the mantras we live by with attention to how they affect our personal narrative and the legacy one intends to create. The reinforcement of opportunities through problem solving engages the creative mind and inspires the heart's curiosity. Love inspires the creative fire within to discover more fulfilling solutions. Affirmations of compassion and strength to endure fortify access to one's will power and support the heart-mind relationship to stay intact and focused. These types of mantras help one design their own legacy of love, reminding one of their authentic self when the experience of burn out, disillusionment, or loss occur.

The practice of mantra awareness and mantra building initiates one onto the path of sovereignty. On this path a sense of responsibility to self, how self is a big factor in the cause and effect of life circumstances, and what imprints one leaves in the world with others becomes central to the everyday experience. This path is one that teaches how to wield the power of self, conscientiously, in order to attain a higher sense of fulfillment that comes when we are liberated from the slavery of ignorance. This ignorance includes subconscious imprinting, behavioral defaults, and old mental or emotional tapes that no longer apply as one discovers new skills to utilize in life events. We all carry ignorance in different ways inside our being. It is a part of this journey to expanding the awareness of self and the relationship of self to the world. That is why compassion and empathy are essential components of healthy connection.

Many teachings in the path of sovereignty challenge an individual to assess the experience of self-sacrifice and martyrdom. How to embrace the balance between fate and free will is a persistent undertone when awakening to sovereignty within. The choice for sovereignty cannot succeed without the acknowledgment of interdependency one has with the environment around self and how that environment influences and reflects the limitations of incarnation back to them. If one seeks a legacy of love, the awareness of this balance is even more integral for allowing mutual exchange between self and other incarnate beings, human or otherwise.

Choices for self-sacrifice or martyrdom occur on all paths of life. Self-sacrifice is chosen when the fixation on a belief or essential need is given up for the sake of a desired outcome. Self-sacrifice may be intentional or unintentional until one becomes aware of what they are doing and how it affects circumstantial outcomes for self and others. This act of self-sacrifice may be a noble act or may be driven by a sense of bondage to personal belief, the pursuit of ideals, or another person. When bondage with self-sacrifice occurs, the role of martyr may be instilled and further a disconnection from the authentic self. When beliefs or emotions are held onto relentlessly, martyrdom occurs at all costs. Many times, the cost may be more than necessary. Only the martyr can be the one to discern this. The compulsion toward martyrdom may also be intentional or unintentional until one becomes aware of how their choices in circumstances cause the outcomes that unfold. When the impulse for martyrdom and self-sacrifice arises, one must re-assess their values and their default coping mechanisms to achieve the outcome they seek.

Is the fixation of an idea or feeling, whether momentary or perpetual, in alignment with the authentic self? Does it deny or defer one's sense of integrity? Does the act of self-sacrifice or martyrdom actually create what we seek most in the intention for holistic fulfillment? The resonance of holistic fulfillment in body, heart, mind, and soul is a hard one to achieve when at odds with one's authentic self. This is also true when an individual relinquishes essential needs for those of another. Is this what love means to us?

Through religious indoctrination and societal fundamentalism we are taught that self-sacrifice is the greatest act of love one can offer. We are also taught one must be willing to die for what they believe in, in order to be self-righteous. These beliefs may have merit in extreme situations such as emergencies, disasters, or acts of persecution. This includes when offenses are made with the purpose of total conversion and conformity that is contrary to the authentic self. Yet how these behaviors ripple out in the everyday experience may not be serving us in the short or long term. Acts of self-sacrifice may not be truly beneficial in all situations for others we offer our bequeathing to. Value systems and the awareness of trade-offs create a negotiation about what one is willing to accept or what one is willing to do to achieve contentment in the body, heart, mind, and soul. As one navigates the situational experiences of life, the common denominator is the self. Unintentional behaviors and impulses to reach contentment often result in only partial satisfaction for the physical body, emotional body, or mental body. Achieving basic life needs for survival may be satisfied, but with the trade-off of beliefs and values. Likewise, emotional desires may be met as a trade-off for basic needs that are not met. It may also be that mental, emotional, and physical contentment is perceived but the spirit feels restless. We all must find our own way in the paths of life through the beliefs, ideals, fears, and struggles to achieve fulfillment.

There are many ways to experience and share love. How we place conditions on love, structures the way we share it with ourselves and with others. Love creates a potent bond, fortifies memories to cherish, enables receptivity for healing, and fuels the integration of personal growth in an elevating way. How one tends to the love they create is reflected by the relationship with oneself, others, and what one seeks to cultivate in the world. Love may be applied in the moments of discontent and suffering an individual perceives on their life path. It may be given directly or indirectly to those that do not understand our love or to those who take on adversarial roles in our journey.

Love flows until it is put into form or rejected from an experience. Circumstance sets the stage and conditions placed on love, by those involved, are the governors of what someone gives or receives from that experience. Compassionate forms of love can teach us how to embrace an experience and how to cultivate non-attachment to fixations of desire when separation or endings occur. When a legacy of love is chosen, one intends to resolve disharmony to maintain connection or seeks closure for release that resonates with compassion and gratitude for the shared experience. Someone with deep abiding love and gratitude in their heart embraces all experiences as opportunities to grow. They understand this is the way to tend to the essence of love for self, others, and the world.

Learning and utilizing a balance of surrendering to fate with intentional choice enables the acceptance for being incarnate as a co-creative being. Acknowledging the way mantras are created through experiences, as well as the way one resonates with thoughtforms shared with us by others, allows the option to use these mantras intentionally. It also allows us to discard them when they are no longer in service to the path of awakening more deeply into the authentic self. Mantras carry the ability to perpetuate experiences in life that do or do not help one achieve holistic fulfillment in body, heart, mind, and soul. It is up to us to re-assess the investment we have in thoughts and feelings that loop in the mind, heart, and soul. Are these thoughts and feelings based in love, compassion, and gratitude for self, life, and others? Do our behaviors and communications in everyday life align with positive receptivity for experiential growth, healing resolutions, and passionate endurance? What legacy are you creating? What legacy do you care to intentionally leave as a mark or a story for yourself in the lives of others here witnessing you?

When an individual chooses the path of sovereignty, they choose the responsibility of awareness and empowerment in order to expand their skills to create in the world. Holding sacred the alignment with one's authenticity cultivates love, compassion, and gratitude for self to share with others from a place of strength and enduring integrity. The key to sharing this is a willingness to be vulnerable with an open heart and trusting in the resilience that is bestowed by practicing lightheartedness in times of hardship. This path presents the opportunity for profound discernment when the impulses for self-sacrifice or martyrdom arise. Experiences of resolve and completion are more likely as one navigates their personal narrative with intentional awareness. By refining beliefs, ideals, values, and behaviors we effect experiential outcomes.

~ The mantras we live by and act from have the power to lead us into bondage or to set us free. Choose your mantras wisely. Choose love as a legacy. ~

X

Choosing Love as a Legacy: Part 2

The perceptions we cultivate about love as an individual and society define the way one gives and receives love. The diverse forms of love are revealed in the roles one takes on in life, the behaviors they act out in relationship with self or others, and the ideals they espouse in their yearnings for fulfillment. The concepts of love that one welcomes in to experience expands a deeper awareness of the inherent force of love. This grants the opportunity to redefine one's relationship to it through free will. The relationship to love an individual defines in self dictates the narratives of connection, creativity, and openness to the emotional experiences of life. How open one is to the experience of love and life affects the legacy they leave behind when the viability of active relationships and the physical body come to an end.

Being open to love as a force of existence inspires the soul to create and to share what is created. The most simplistic example of this is the desire to be "one" with another and choose the opportunity to create a child together (or to raise one together if physical gestation is not applicable). The inspiration to create that is fueled by love, in many forms, may be limitless in the mind and heart. This is because the empowerment of birthing and tending energy furthers the questions of possibility. It may also be confined and structured by intentions and beliefs that seek to contain it in a specific form to achieve a focused outcome. Whether the resistance and conditional structures are healthy or unhealthy for those involved is up to the assessment of those cultivating it. Although, observers may also conclude their own view of it without choosing to create the same experience in their own personal narrative. Navigating the emotional experience in that expression of love and free will is a part of learning and growth for how we manifest our dreams in alignment with the authentic self.

Love and free will are partners in the acts of creativity that are endeavored in life. The way an individual harnesses the power of free will is directly relevant to the outcomes and productivity of their experiences. Maintaining the use of free will as a skill that supports resilience with an open heart and a curiosity to learn, perpetuates the probabilities for fulfillment. Mastering receptivity to love, learning, and creative potential perpetuates the momentum of evolution and the cyclical return of lightheartedness through perceptions of hardship. Resistance, denial, avoidance, and aggressive acts of destruction shut down the flow of creativity and dampen the power of love as a resource. Individuals exercising their free will to defend, control, or obscure the possibilities that do not fit the mold of their current understandings and beliefs are choosing to step out of the creative flow of life. This directly affects them and others in relationship with them. While this may be an important lesson in the use of free will and allows one to get their bearings on how to learn and embrace life beyond unhealthy circumstances, living one's life this way consistently leads to a perceived lack of fulfillment. This choice may also harbor persistent beliefs driven by fear, anger, resentment, or regret that block opportunities for creative solutions and growth. Creative solutions expand one's capacity for resilience with an open heart and ultimate fulfillment.

When the acts of love one seeks to share with another or the world is denied, deferred, or unacknowledged the choice to still allow and tend to that love arises. The power of unconditional love and the freedom an individual feels to experience this form of love resonates and ripples through time, regardless of an actualized or currently shared relationship to other(s). This love is the essence of compassionate acceptance that we all have diverse paths and ways we create that shift the definitions of self, relationship, and the nature of our experiential world. The conditionality of one's love is revealed when they cut off the flow and recognition of that love within themselves and toward another they once shared love with. When roles change, dreams are fulfilled, or experiences feel unfulfilling, the forms of conditional love change. At this time, it is not uncommon for cognitive dissonance to occur because we each crave unconditional love. Yet, the perceived tightening or release of conditions on the roles we play in relationship or that we place on ourselves for our endeavors in the external world require a recalibration of how one distributes their mental, emotional, and physical energy. The focus of the mind and heart may become consumed with immediate gratification. This affects the choices an individual makes that hold gravity later in reflections of life experience, personal performance, and the legacy one has imprinted in the psyche of others and oneself. This is important to understand when considering choices that will result in mundane or transformative themes in the experience of life and the legacy one has the power to create.

The theme of a legacy is marked by intentional awareness of the way our experience imprints on others and the effect of karmic narratives woven into the journey of soul. The value of a legacy for self is an essential part of accessing free will to master how we are molded by life experience and how we create with our own life force. Learning how to align with greater integrity in our words and actions produces greater opportunities for fulfillment, healing, and closure in every aspect of how we relate to life experience and relationships to others. Even if others cannot meet us there or maintain the open flow of love and healthy communication, it is our devotion to the integrity of love, of oneself, and the legacy we are cultivating that fortifies the creativity and sustainability of love in this earthly embodiment.

The conditions of love may take on diverse forms that invite new perceptions of love and definitions for the roles we take on to experience that love. Life is a journey of lessons by experiences directly or vicariously. Different people share this journey with us as we establish connection in all its meanings and refine how we align during the challenges of existence. These challenges invite us to evolve in our understandings of how we automatically and voluntarily direct the narratives experienced and shared. They also affect how we align with ourselves and who we choose to align with. This may cause the dissolution of relationships we once valued if one or both individuals do not seek to maintain or redefine the perceived love that was shared.

The love we carry for others cannot be forced on them if they are not open to receive. That is why offerings and invitations are the messengers of love. If the impulse is to force love or shut down the flow of love for another, one must look to their free will and the nature of the love they carry for others. Is it conditional or unconditional? Is it both in some ways? Do you have the reservoir and the will to still love that being even if they cannot receive or understand your offerings and invitations? Offerings and invitations leave messages at the door of those who are closed to you. Sometimes moving on with appreciation for what was shared with them is the healthiest path for self. Accepting that truth may look different to more than one individual at any given time, without needing to demonize it or degrade someone for it, is a foundational tool for reaching emotional freedom. This includes valuing the dreams they brought into your life even if you were unable to experience that dream with them. It is important to remember the endings of our involvements, in anything or with anyone, in life are equally valuable to the beginnings. All of the acts in a journey from beginning to end are a reflection of the self we are choosing in life. Having integrity with healthy communication for release offers a productive path to resolving and healing the grief that naturally resonates with endings.

Love is its own force. To choose a legacy of love means to love regardless of whether your love is received. It is a perpetual connection to the unconditional nature of love's essence, the power of creativity, and the potentiation of evolution that must be embraced to act in the integrity of love as a life force. Love is a skillful practice to master during this embodiment. Love teaches us to deepen our knowledge of self, of others, and the power of shared connection for co-creativity. Love is the song that brings us home, that inspires a new day, and fuels the will to be present in every moment. Love teaches us how to communicate more effectively with oneself and others, to have compassion when we are not understood, and to find graceful approaches to release pain and endings. Applying this understanding secures future possibilities to share in new ways that serve and align with the authentic self.

~ Love is the reminder of the spark of creativity within you. You hold that key. You hold the access to the love and the creative power within you, regardless of the narratives you witness or the stories you tell yourself. It is up to you to choose a legacy of love and gratitude, no matter what. ~

XI

⧯∞⧯

Queries and Theories on Karmic Debt

What is karma? How do we know it exists? If something bad or good happens to us, is it simply because of previous karma we created? Is fate truly so intertwined with every decision we make? The Buddhist philosophy of karma is not the only spiritual belief system that suggests an indebtedness to the choices one makes. It just happens to be the origin of the most common term used in today's spiritual conversations within the Western world. Karma may also be called retribution, consequence, the law of returns, or nature's justice, etc. It may be likened to Hammurabi's code, "an eye for an eye- a tooth for a tooth" and fatalistic thinking that reinforces a lack of control or a sense of guilt. What is the true balance of personal choice and that which is beyond one's control? Do we become the purveyors of karma and consequence or does some greater force beyond us cause it? These questions commonly arise when life is going great or when life brings hardship. They appear in the stream of consciousness within that seeks to know- what is life? What is it all for? Why me?

If you pick up any religious text or mythological account, arche-types, allegories, and aphorisms fill the pages with reflections of truth and the laws of human existence. These texts are an attempt to portray the many teachings the mystics, sages, and priesthoods have witnessed in time. Their truths can be edified over and over in the acceptance and reiteration of generational belief cultivated through-out thousands of years. In an individual's personal journey for truth, ignoring, questioning, and denying these conclusions and stories of the past are natural responses to defining one's own destiny. The child within wants to know more than it is being told. It seeks the unknown with inherent curiosity, sometimes to the point of chaos and endangerment. That is, it's nature. We all carry this inner child as a reflection of our inner spark for life, not just the story of how we grew into our physical age. Becoming an adult is a journey of self-discovery that requires exploration of knowledge, beliefs, and direct experience. The way one embraces, rejects, or toes the line of these informational opportunities, frames the perception of one's identity. Anyone's life may be shared and written as an allegory or example of the truth they observed or that others perceive about their experience from the outside. Perhaps, the point of life and questions about fate resolve in the act of witnessing one's story.

Witnessing one's story requires subjective and objective self-awareness. Then, by seeing the choices one has made and plans to make, an individual may experience a sense of power to change or create their own personal narrative. The will to power thrives from the instinct to survive. Yet, when the needs of basic survival are met, that willpower expands into higher aspirations. Humankind has evolved a very different set of circumstances over time, allowing the brain to develop higher order functions that still rely on instinct, yet now supersede it with ideals and innovations. When an individual harnesses the will to affect their own story and the outcomes of their behaviors, that individual enters into a conversation with fate, karma, and intention. Fate is defined as a greater power beyond one's control or a pre-written experience one must yield to. Karma is defined as the debt or consequence, whether beneficial or detrimental to the perception of life lessons and soul fulfillment. Intention is the discernment of choice and behaviors that arise from self-awareness to empower the unfolding of outcomes in order to change or co-create with one's perceived fate or karma.

Fatalistic thinking gifts the individual the option to surrender to life and self as it is, yet also enables a lack of accountability in the deferral of one's willpower to perceive and act differently through the cultivation of self-awareness. There are many fantasies and horrors to enrapture the mind when it comes to living by the will of something greater than oneself. Fate, like karma and intention, is a powerful teacher about the forces beyond oneself. It reminds us to have humility for what we do not know and that we are not the masters of the universe. Fate reminds us we are merely a part of it, another story to be written among the billions of stars shining into infinity.

Karmic debts and returns are the scales between fate and intentional willpower. The law of attraction for what one puts out into the world, directs at others, and propagates in oneself is assumed to return the same energy in kind. How an individual values these payoffs and consequences perpetuates the ripple effects of choice and personal surrender in their personal narrative. The cycles of karma may be relevant to an individual's experience of connection through beautiful and challenging relationships with family, lovers, friends, or colleagues. Current life patterns or past life stories may arise as an echo or de ja vu' sensation as the interactions of the story unfold. Levels of understanding and intention to perceive a situation or to act differently begin to awaken, reveal, resolve, and dissolve karma felt from the past. This is a conscious and unconscious experience. The more conscious it is, the more intention one may empower to service the call for healing and completion around the internal and external struggles of this chapter in their story. When karmic completions occur, the storyline of a life shifts with the deepened sense of connection an individual feels to how it has or will define them. The release of karmic debts opens new doorways in the wisdom of one's identity and embodied power to create something new in the next chapter of their personal narrative.

The power of intention calls us like the allure of a magician's wand. The will to create and direct one's life is a natural urge that is often nourished or challenged by an individual's circumstances and the people they share life with. The desire lurks beneath the surface of the psyche to change the hard things and invoke the good things in life, even under the pretentious beliefs of engrained guilt and shame. Seeking the power of intention requires cultivating a balance between surrendering to fate and learning to resolve karmic debts or repetitive patterns that hinder one's perception of empowered fulfillment. Some may say to be intentional is a way to seek control over an experience. Being intentional may exhibit malevolent or benevolent desires, effects, and outcomes depending on the perception of power in the world and self. Intention can create karma as much as it can resolve it. When life feels beyond one's control the natural response is to attempt to control some part of the experience, ourselves, or others. Benevolent intention is more about creative manifestation than control from a place of arrogance or authority. When we try to control life and others, we create power struggles that may originate in karmic stories or become karmic debt. Intention honors the autonomy of power within and the power of forces outside of us. It means aligning the ability one holds to affect their own internal state, exhibited through behaviors and choices, while formulating requests, invitations, and offerings to the external powers that influence us and life. Intention is a tool for transformation. It fortifies an individual's authentic self beyond the nuances of karmic roles and stage setting filters. It embraces a power beyond oneself in this life and many lives after, whether in heaven, hell, earth, or some other realm altogether. At the very least, it assists one in achieving a more fulfilling and empowered experience of the life you are writing now.

It is your choice to perceive the power of fate, karma, and intention. The story continues to unfold with each thought, each action, and each breath. Where is your attention? Can you see yourself? Can you feel the power within to create with life and transform? Self-awareness and motivation for enduring resolutions grants you the freedom to evolve and excel at the game we call life. Let your inner child seek the healing it requires and the impassioned curiosity to know the power of its own illumination. This is the core of all spiritual texts that define "awakening."

- Take a chance with fate. Bargain for your karma if you find it appealing or complete the contracts that bind you. You hold the pen to write your own destiny, to surrender in your own way, and to embrace, perpetuate, and resolve your own karma. Your heart is the feather to be weighed on the scales of truth in this journey of soul. -

XII

⁘

The Masks We Wear and the Filters We Construct

Life is filled with pre-designed constructs for who to be and how to be that we all fall into. Even the trend of being "an unfiltered, raw individual" is a construct that sets expectation but does not require looking deeper at who we really are and why we say the things we say or do the things we do. As human civilization has changed over time, so have the principles we are taught or influenced by through varying circles of socialization. The truth is we all want to belong, no matter how much we strive to be a pioneer of individualism. Any moment may bring the perceived pressure to mask one's true feelings or thoughts, in order to sustain connection. These moments may be inconsequential or prove to be monumental in how one's experiences of fulfillment or lack fulfillment further unfold.

"You can't be honest all the time", "Fake it till you make it", are common advice and justifications from role models and peers over the generations. The average person lies 1-2 times a day, according to polls completed year over year. It seems evident that white lies are acceptable to most but how many white lies add up to a total face change? Are white lies a gateway to bigger lies? How many big lies does one have to tell before they have forgotten their authentic self? Masks, make-up, photo filters, life filters all create a sense of beauty, idealism, perfection, and what is deemed more acceptable. Adhering to the ideals of perfection on the outside does not resolve the denial of truth on the inside. True contentment will always be just beyond reach if we do not choose introspection on the values we seek to uphold and healing around the pieces of self we commonly ignore, deny, band-aid, or make callous. The less self-aware we are, the more impulsive and reactive we become. The less development and cultivation one pursues, in the truth of who they really are and whether that is aligned with their statements and actions, the more illusion, folly, and discontent one creates in their life story. A disconnection with one's authentic self only preserves and perpetuates unsatisfying connections with others because illusions are fragile. Every mask, no matter how well it is artfully constructed to deceive and endure, falls in the face of the greatest opportunities and hardships life brings.

Masks and filters are different. Masks are an illusion or an ideal an individual projects in order to belong, receive short-term gratification, and hide the more vulnerable inner workings of the mind, heart, and soul. Filters are constructed from our reactions to experiences and indoctrination from societal institutions or familial foundations. Filters may be conscious or unconscious in the heart and mind. Filters on a soul level may also be innate programming from previous incarnations or ancestral wounds that are yet to be healed or re-defined. It is natural in the course of life to try on masks and filters as a means to understanding the human experience, belief constructs, and the pursuit of one's perceived wants and needs. At this time in human history, the intermixing of cultures, remote digital interactions, and the demands of what is "perceived success" provide a banquet of material and social attraction in abundance that is laid within a minefield of judgment, competition, conformity, persecution, and many other pitfalls or hurdles. The demand of the achievement is that of perfection in your final landing in order to eat at the table, but this is an illusion. It is an illusion projected by a runaway mind that does not know its own heart. No journey is perfect, otherwise we wouldn't have the notion of progress. Even when an individual reaches some sense of perfection, there is always some way they could have done it better, according to others. If one has to sacrifice the truth of their own identity to meet the demands or desires of others, is this truly perfection? Whose happiness are we concerned with and how many masters are we serving in order to serve ourselves?

The truth of this can only be found in the sorting and clarifying of the masks we wear and the filters we use to dictate how we give to and receive from others. Filters create pre-formed expectations. These expectations will inevitably shift throughout the learning inherent in a life story by trial and error or through the dedication of mindfulness in one's intentions. How do avoidance, disregard, and denial serve the truth of your own heart? The mind may find momentary peace or opportunity but the heart waits to be seen, growing more and more quiet and hidden, like a neglected or abused child. When the heart is forced into this state again and again, the spark for life becomes less and less tangible. Depression and anxiety are direct responses to the way one is not fulfilling the requirements of the authentic self, and building trust in the heart to be seen and tended. They are responses to unfiltered honesty the mind continues to defer for the illusion of self-protection, in lieu of the opportunity to heal. The way to fulfill the needs of the authentic self, heart, and mind is to accept accountability with compassionate communication and intentional transparency to align personal values with statements and behaviors. Honoring the authentic self and surrendering the requirement of others to perform or provide something for you invites one to harness the capacity for self-reliance, rooted in self-love, as well as compassion to the limitations of others. From here, one expands the perception of beauty and intrigue creating the most enduring and real face to share with the world. No mask required.

The more masks and filters we construct our life with, the less healing and karmic resolve we achieve in order to redefine or truly live our own authentic destiny. The path of sovereignty does not dictate aloneness nor require a refusal to belong. Sovereignty of the heart and soul offers the mind true freedom from cyclical victimhood, martyrdom, complacency, the scatter of confusion, and carrying the burdens of others' demands, desires, or beliefs when they negate or deny the needs of the authentic self. The freedom to meet life and share oneself with an open, resilient heart and soulful integrity is the path to fulfillment. Bowing down to the fear of separation and no longer belonging in a relationship, a group, a dream, or a belief system actually creates separation within self and ripples out into those relationships. This is because people inherently seek authenticity and honesty even when they ask you to be what they want you to be for them. There is a disconnect in that demand as much as there is a disconnect within self, pretending or trying to meet it. It is an illusion that we could ever ignore forever who we really are at our heart of hearts and what we need to be fulfilled. This is where weighing the value of wants versus needs is imperative in order to discern the gravity of trade-offs when responding consciously to opportunities for belonging that challenge the integrity of the authentic self. Much of the journey is about learning what we need to be fulfilled and where we feel we belong, but it is common for people to settle for less due to the fear of separation or of challenging the filters they use to define a comfort zone.

Discernment, honorable transparency, compassionate communication, and healthy boundaries are essential skills to maintaining integrity with self, relationships, and life endeavors. Acknowledging that we are all on a path to learning, healing, and evolving beyond karmic contracts and historical influences, in order to refine the experience of embodiment, supports a balance of perspective when conflict, judgment, and separation occurs. Becoming a witness of self and a witness of others may be used for personal or collective gain, depending on the intentional choices made from the knowledge of these observations. Being honest and sovereign does not mean raw projection of judgmental attitudes, superiority, or demanding others comply with your needs or boundaries. It is a practice of being clear in oneself about what you must choose in order to maintain healthy boundaries, how to find alignments with oneself to life and people that fulfill your mind and heart, and nourish self-integrity. Choosing sovereignty for self and respecting the inherent sovereignty of others aligns with the release of a need to control others or the outcomes of events. Being intentional is not about controlling and manipulating. Intentional living is about defining what we have the power to shift within oneself in order to affect one's perceptions of an outcome. The practice of surrender is as much an integral part of reaching fulfillment, as are the directive behaviors of intention. Life is about co-creation with circumstance and others involved. A soulful path is not about dominion, superiority, or acting for the sake of perfection to pull off an illusion. It is about sorting, reflecting, respecting, and the process of refinement that aligns us to what is real and valuable.

- Cradle the sacred spark of your inner child. Dive deep into the well to discover the truth of your own heart. Quiet the mental antics that parade the illusion of safety. Reach beyond the comfort zone of what you think you know and silence the talking heads of society to discern the essential requirements of a radiant soul. Your path is your own and you belong with those who honor the integrity of who you are becoming. -

XIII

⬥

Establishing Self-Authority

When we enter the world for the first time, we are helpless and fragile infants. We are fully dependent on our mother, father, or guardian to nourish and protect us until we can learn the skills to forage, defend, and survive on our own. This process of development is multilayered and may be interrupted or impacted throughout that process. Developing the instincts and the skills for physical survival is foundational to progressing in emotional and mental arenas that present different challenges for a greater sense of fulfillment. In the human experience, these layers of development begin to enfold and intertwine with one another as conscious awareness of life circumstances and opportunities expand beyond the age of 3. By the age of 2 and 3, a child discovers the word "No", but does not quite understand the use of it to establish self-authority. This age also begins to develop self-direction and more complex communication of demands for perceived needs and wants. The capacity for self-authority is defined throughout the journey of life circumstances and how an individual learns to respond to the inner voice of self and the voices of others they share life with. Establishing true self-authority requires progressive degrees of autonomy through self-reflection and sovereignty through intentional choices that are founded in self-knowing and personal empowerment.

In order to establish progressive mastery in one's self-authority, the active introspection and curiosity for one's thoughts, emotions, and behaviors they inherently accept as their identity must be applied. This active witnessing shows the contradictions, distortions, discomfort, and poor justifications that naturally occur in one's interactions with self and non-self. It also reveals the truth of desire, the urge to idealism, the focus of satisfaction through justification, and the uplifting sensation of synchronized authenticity. Discerning and weighing the behaviors, thoughts, and emotions that are truly ours, requires the process of rooting out the source of these imprints in one's childhood, family and friend group, partner alliance, or generational and societal overtones. Through this discernment the compass for self-love and honoring the value of one's truth, whether different or parallel to these outer influences, aligns with the greatest path of development and expression of an individual's authentic self.

When an individual aligns with the integrity of their true nature, deep beliefs, and aspirations, they unlock the doors of their own personal maze. They build an indestructible bridge to the center of self, the core of the will and of self-definition, the reservoir of power through acknowledgment, and wisdom through self-love and self-accountability. These are the skills that define a strong and temperate leader. Becoming a strong and temperate leader of one's own life through the observation of thoughts, the honoring of emotions, and the governance of your expressed behaviors, expands the quality of opportunities to experience confidence, justice, and mutual fulfillment when giving and receiving with others in the pursuit of life endeavors.

The concept of "re-parenting" and "adulting" have become buzz words in today's psychological focus and general group interactions. These very personal judgments and perceptions of one's parents, peers, or self that are expressing trauma response behaviors due to abuse, neglect, abandonment, and smothering, are now a growing societal conversation. Admitting or acknowledging one's perceptions of immaturity is becoming easier, yet the question remains for each individual of how to define "What is mature enough for them?" and "How do they shift their behaviors to be in alignment and loyalty to their clarified truth without resenting how they discovered that truth?"

Establishing self-authority is a singular relationship with one's personal truth that supports how they navigate their own choices in life. It is not about dominion or wielding justice over anyone else's truth, behaviors, or choices. The point is to execute good leadership for self and apply that to other positions of authority, one may be placed in or achieve in community and society, without a double standard. This requires the adherence of discernment for how to honor the integrity of self and others, instead of the arrogance and dismissal of dignity that judgment displays. When an individual holds onto strong judgments about others, they disregard that person's creative potential to honor their own self-authority and whatever circumstances, imprints of belief, and value of behaviors have served them in surviving their life story up to that point. Mistakes, judgments, impulses, and strategic choices are a part of the human experience in the path of developing and refining conscious awareness as an individual and a collective. It is what an individual does with these attributes that affects the power of self-authority.

The deepest wisdom that fortifies the power of self-authority is that, "you are the only one you have power over", when it comes to defining loyalties at the core of oneself. This includes what one can change in their own personal narrative, the choices to re-orient how energy is invested, and how one navigates the co-creation of life with others.

When one has children, the opportunity to teach and mimic good leadership skills in order to impart a strong foundation to build their child's self-authority, temperance, and accountability, is the most profound offering a parent may give beyond the gift of life itself. If an individual feels this was not given to them, it must be an active choice to learn how to do so, in order to impart it to their own offspring. No matter when it occurs, the journey to establishing self-authority brings deep healing and priceless wisdom to work with life and others in more graceful ways through the strength of authenticity. Even if an individual does not have children their willingness to embark on this healing and clarifying journey to reach self-authority can be witnessed as an example to all others they come into contact, conflict, and relationship with. These interactions have ripple effects in the collective as we each feel the influence and observe the creative power of identity in others.

When we acknowledge that our inner child will always be a part of us and embrace the curiosity and open heartedness that young children remind us of, as well as nourish the parts of that inner child to become sovereign in alignment with the spirit of their true nature, we are freeing that child within to walk their own path with the permission to discover something new. This "new something" is how consciousness in the human experience expands its capacity and exhibits the higher degrees of maturity we vaguely define as "becoming an adult." Defining the adult within and choosing to continually meet more and more of oneself is how we co-create more fulfilling outcomes. It is how one restores joy in the connection between our child self and adult self when life experiences separate or diffuse the power of this inner relationship.

~ Turn and face your inner child. Embrace the longings and the pain. Acknowledge the connection between your younger and elder self. Heal through establishing self-authority and loyalty to the integrity of who you have always believed you are at the center of the maze. Walk back to your true nature in times of conflict to re-assess the map before leading yourself onward. Hold sacred the co-creative power we each carry to define our own destiny, alone or together, generation by generation. ~

XIV

⤜⤛

The Proper Use of Power

In the reductionist thinking of the mind, power is many things. It is a tool or a weapon, a feeling or a knowing, something within and outside of us. Acknowledging the role of power is to recognize the effects of raw creativity. It starts with instinct, a sense of compulsion to do something with our body, then objects, and later with people. As we learn what it is and how to use it, the hierarchy of power encodes itself in the heart and mind as willpower, self-empowerment, power in authority outside of us, power struggles, collaborative power in connection and relationship, the power to create or transform, and the power to manipulate or destroy. Power is a raw experience channeled through intention to become a force of nature. This force affects our sense of self and our lives in every way.

When we activate a sense of power, it is further defined by our will to use it as a tool or a weapon. The experience of power and the active force of it may be hard or soft in one's applications.

Knowing when to hold one's ground, circulating power within, and when to direct that power outward is an essential lesson in the journey of life. Circumstances arise that require one or both ways of managing power and the outcomes that result reveal to us whether our intentions have succeeded. Outcomes also show how the use of power was lacking in delivery for effect and if one's perception of power has caused a backlash in some way. Reflecting on these outcomes can improve precision through problem-solving and discernment in order to apply creative solutions for restoring a balance of power. Learning the proper use of power is essential to affect and create more fulfilling outcomes in one's endeavors in the world and one's perception of sustainable empowerment in the face of things beyond their control. Elders, gurus, spiritual teachers, and acclaimed thought influencers consistently speak on the need to understand the proper use of power. This is achieved through applied pragmatism.

Accepting what an individual has the power to change within oneself, in order to affect change in their personal narrative and in the external world, is a teaching in pragmatism. Harnessing one's power for the good of self and the good of others is another. Often, power struggles arise due to the inability of a person to see the perspective of the other and sustain receptivity to mutual solutions that empower both individuals or groups. Emotional self-absorption, irrational mindsets lacking acuity and focus, and assertions of power to portray or embed an authoritative role are all factors that instigate power struggles. This may occur within the mind of an individual or between individuals or groups. The focus on preferred outcomes or a sense of resolve must be maintained or power loss through the scatter of competing emotions and mental rationale will inevitably occur. Power dynamics are based on give and take. Acknowledging what one has to give without depleting their own sense of foundational empowerment is important when assessing the balance of give and take in an argument, relationship, or creative endeavor. Understanding that we each have different capacities to carry and deliver power is also an important part of evaluating power dynamics. However, an individual's current capacity for power does not limit them from the expansion of that capacity in the journey of learning how to nourish and work with their own power.

When safeguarding one's sense of power, the discernment of wants and needs, perceptions of essential values, and factors that reduce a sense of integrity with self must be evaluated. When a feeling of depletion or exhaustion occurs, it is necessary to reflect and tend to empowerment within through nourishing outlets or practices. These may include exercise, time in nature, shared time with uplifting and supportive people, researching other perspectives that inspire, tending to bodily needs with cleansing practices and power foods. Reclaiming one's power when it feels taken or depleted by others or a creative endeavor, requires an individual to set boundaries, know when to say "no", and to discontinue a relationship or endeavor if a fulfilling flow of give and take is denied or unable to be reached. Most often, reclaiming power requires that an individual first honor boundaries and needs within self, in order to uphold them with others. This is imperative to learn for those often stuck in co-dependent, neglectful, or abusive relationships and for individuals who have a history of feeling like a doormat for others, a victim, or unacknowledged for their merits, offerings, and strengths. If an individual denies the opportunities to cultivate power within, they will remain in victim and childlike roles without self-authority, recognition, and autonomy. This will perpetuate the attraction of relationships with others that control, abuse, or neglect an individual, compounding their perceptions of weakness, helplessness, and foolishness. This pattern eventually generates the persona of a "hungry soul" seeking to claim power from others for self through the same ego tactics of condescension and intimidation for control, abuse, and neglect.

Power is life force. It bestows a sense of vitality in one's daily experience and relationships. To be alive is to have the capacity to carry and utilize power. Power exists within. The power outside oneself exists in other beings and natural elements that manifest in the earth and universe. Being a witness for how others use their power, in order to respond effectively with your own is how one maintains self-authority and refrains from depleting power struggles. "Know when to hold'em, fold'em, or play'em" is effectively learned through acknowledging others capacity to hold, utilize, and share power as well as the discernment of context and circumstance when evaluating how to wield one's own power. Honorable transparency, compassionate communication, and trusting in one's resilience with an open mind and an open heart, are the skills that may be cultivated by wielding one's power with intention and mindful awareness. Mindful awareness challenges one's perceptions to seek pragmatic view-points, in order to learn when to apply one's power inwardly or outwardly. Distinguishing how one's perceptions serve the ego or the soul of the authentic self, further refines the raw power one carries and cultivates.

The more an individual defines and utilizes their power with confidence in self-authority, the more challenges may arise from others who seek to gain or affect that power for themselves. This is especially true for those who are in situations and relationships with "hungry souls" or a significant imbalance of power. These challenges to an individual's power will attempt to test it, muddle it, or take it. When this occurs, an individual that has come to understand the nature of power and the proper use of power will acknowledge the illusion these challenges present and overcome any fear of losing their own power of self-authority or giving up power that would damage their integrity with self. To be clear, foregoing the opportunity to assert one's power with others is not the act of giving up power if an individual chooses to assert that power within themselves for an intentional outcome that supports the authentic self. This is relative to the balance of power perceived when a struggle initiates the need for choice in the proper use of power.

Hard power and soft power are both useful and have trade-offs for the outcomes one seeks. Pushing one's need over another's is the use of hard power. Choosing a firm boundary with another attempting to intimidate and control you is also hard power. Soft power is wielded through vocalization or quiet acceptance of another's position, in contrast to your own without pushing arguments about that difference. Soft power may also be an active choice to go along with someone's request when it doesn't challenge an individual's integrity and does not give up an essential need perceived by the ego or the soul. All individuals have their own path of discovery to walk, in order to understand their own power and how to apply it. The way one individual applies soft or hard power may be very different than another. Establishing the intention for mutual resolve and honoring the integrity of all involved will influence the creative capacity for all individuals to balance a perceived power dynamic, relative to the circumstances. Sharing power means negotiating a path to fulfill the primary needs of those involved. The more we, as a collective, align with the deeper needs of the ego self and the soul beyond the superficial layers of impulse and egoic desires, the more profound the wielding of power may become.

When life demands instigate internal or external conflict,

default behaviors, unhealthy compensatory habits, and mental, emotional, physical, and spiritual fatigue may occur. The more demands at one time, the more likely these will occur in combination or totality. This is when power within self may feel compromised or waning in sustainability. It is also when the capacity of one's power can be expanded and wielded in new innovative ways. The seed of power exists within and will always have the power to grow, no matter how depleted one believes they are. It is belief that structures an individual's capacity and belief that effects one's endurance. "Nothing can happen to me that is bigger than I am" may be interpreted as "Anything that happens to me is within my capacity to find a creative way to resolve."   Belief in oneself and honoring one's power is essential to endure the challenges of life experiences. To honor one's power, an individual must have self-love and self-respect. They must be able to reflect and discern the origins of their intentions and desires that lead to their behaviors. One must be able to embrace accountability and realize the power within self to choose effectively for the soul's fulfillment, in balance with basic needs and egoic desires. Every choice has trade-offs. Discernment of the most valuable trade-offs is essential to feeling empowered by a choice. This is how an individual actualizes the authentic self and cultivates the proper use of power through life experience.

~ Focus on the seed of power within you to harness innate potential. Cultivate mindfulness and connection to the authentic self, in order to nourish discernment for the balance of power in times of conflict. Embody confidence in your capacity to expand and share empowerment with others through choice. ~

XV

⟨❦⟩

Unearthing the Power of Emotion

As the pendulum swings in life circumstances, one's emotional awareness expands. Challenges perceived turn our senses on or off, which can perpetuate the experience of power and powerlessness, as well as fluidity and inertia. The architectural design of the bridge between one's mind and heart is influenced consistently by their responses to life circumstances. Maintaining a focus on protecting, refining, or rebuilding this bridge is essential in times of conflict, hardship, loss, and the looming unknown. By honoring the deep contemplation that comes with inertia and cultivating decisiveness in the trade-offs of how an experience is serving us, one can restore the flow of informative understanding as a balance is found in the bridge connecting the vast differences of the heart and mind. Emotions can be dulled by the mind through objectivity or become overwhelming when given full immersion in subjectivity. Emotions can be exacerbated or held hostage by our thoughts and beliefs or inform us of a deeper truth in oneself that has been covered up by rationale. Unearthing this deeper truth kept sacred by the heart will always be essential to reaching the experience of closure, resolve, and fulfillment.

People are wired with different biases from their experiences through imprinting in childhood and family constructs, personal exploration of identity apart from involuntary acceptance of belief or validation by others, and through the pursuit of knowledge that one has the power to perceive through cultivating the attributes of sensory awareness. Throughout the formative process of self-identity in this current state of human evolution, a focus on the mind and its power to control, regulate, and create is primary. Many of our practices of self-development require a demanding curriculum of mental marathons, in today's societies. Yet, some of the oldest societies on earth echo the teaching of quieting the mind and reconnecting the body wisdom and/or the heart's intuition. Many practices in religion and spirituality carry these old teachings as well. These practices may or may not be inherently spiritual. The semantics of language and interpretation is another mental antic that divorces one from the power of feeling. Noticing one's bias toward the mind and surrendering to the power of sensory awareness in the body is the only way to cultivate the seeds of intuition. Intuition is the inner knowing that aligns our choices and behaviors toward the most fulfilling path for our personal narrative.

The diversity of human experience and individual processing of life experiences substantiates primary tendencies toward leading one's perceptions with thought or emotion. Some beings are highly specialized in their capacity to sense, feel through, and read the depths of emotional information. Others are specialized in their capacity to explore, structure, and analyze the vast algorithms of mental computation. The beauty of these focused specializations is that chartable maps may be shared for the navigation of understanding and co-creation in human relationships to each other, the global community, and the sentience that earth offers as the container of our existence. The challenge these specializations reveal is the requirement of a bridge designed to uphold, funnel, and filter the multidimensional information both realms of the identified and unidentified self have to share. This bridge enables the most fine-tuned clarity that may be reached in the circumstances that occur in an individual's personal narrative, based in the factual events of life and the context of an individual's perceptual capacity.

The logarithms of emotion and the algorithms of thought for problem-solving and expansion of understanding are fortified through one's use of them. In today's world and the projections of our future, it is paramount to unearth our emotional intelligence and refine emotional regulation, in order to attain and sustain a balanced perspective of our informative experiences, perceptions, and choices. Through the balance of emotional and mental intelligence we reveal a path to healthy practices for well-being. Once a sense of well-being and established self-authority is discovered, an individual may refine this sense of self and personality they harmonize most with in the "I am" experience. When an individual feels lost, removed, or cut off from this "sense of self", they have the resonance of feeling-knowing deep within to seek it out again in order to restore the potency of connection for a refined sense of that self. The mind and body act as assistants for cataloguing the memories of one's sensory awareness. No matter how one seeks to evolve beyond the intensity that the senses may invoke through experiences, the senses are always there informing the mind and body of what is knowable in the physical world one exists in. An individual cannot divide the sacred relationship of body and mind without the other degenerating and becoming less of itself.

When the mind listens to the heart's intuition by way of the body's wisdom, the relevance of thought is empowered for higher accuracy in sorting, releasing, and clarification of perception. Unearthing the power of emotion and cultivating acuity of the senses may be a daunting task to those that lead with distanced rationale, but it is easy to see the whole is not served. Unnecessary strain is put on the system and the outcomes of an endeavor when the general is not listening to the soldiers telling him the map does not match the ground or when supervisors in corporate administration disregard the reality of workers that they are holding the demands over to meet statistical benchmarks because they are in a hypothetical and removed state of mind. A bridge of caring and awareness for what is yet to be known of the moving parts and their capacity to function beyond ideals must be maintained for success in any endeavor or conflict resolution, otherwise anarchy and revolution may occur. The mind must be informed by the senses to understand reality, lest it become a dictator of inconjunct ideologies and cognitive dissonance. It must honor the formed and the formless attributes of emotion to navigate the world with the skill of pragmatism.

The potency and depth of emotional responses can seem as vast as the ocean, perhaps the universe, but emotion is contained in the body which is of the earth, and therefore emotion carries the wisdom of healthy boundary and containment. Like the ocean, emotions ebb and flow. They churn and calm and they shift into our awareness as deep as the light can penetrate for illumination. Sometimes, emotions break their boundaries and wash over, clearing and cleansing the surface of one's consciousness or destroying and renewing the structures of the mind. Sometimes, emotions are so formless in an individual's perception, logic cannot be applied. The attention to facts can be disregarded or denied and the only boundary one feels is the shield they have raised to keep the rest of the world out. This may include their own logarithmic ways to understanding that would offer form to formlessness. These are the moments an individual has dived so deep within that the light of illumination is not penetrating their immersion in the abyss of feeling. When this occurs, those on the outside witnessing can only wait with patience and hope that the other will find a way to communicate effectively with themselves and others again, regardless of the circumstances. The individual immersed in their own abyss must choose the effort and courage required to pull up the pearls from the emotional deep they are seeking and to cleanse and clear the distortions of their own perception with themselves and others for healing. They must choose form beyond formlessness to refine and reconnect the bridge between their mind and heart in order to open the flow of wholeness that enables a sense of closure and fulfillment.

Humanity is a profound characteristic of the human species to be safeguarded. This function of consciousness is revered as a cornerstone in the foundation of our evolution. The bridge of the senses to the mind must be protected if we seek to continue our advancement as a species and as an individual experiencing what it means to live, at all. Seeking the path to establishing self-authority, honorable transparency, and the skill to understand and communicate the multidimensional perceptions of one's heart and mind in a unified sense of self empowers emotional and mental growth, regulation, and the expansion of conscientious intelligence. How do your heart and mind inform you? How do you compensate in the changing circumstances of life to maintain your sense of self?

~ Let your body senses inform your emotional awareness. Allow these emotions to flow across the hemispheres of the mind. Fine-tune the algorithms of your mental filters by walking the bridge to the center of your heart and meet the invitation of holistic feeling-knowing. Uphold the sacredness of your own humanity and persevere through the journey of distortion, refraction, and loss with the courage for clarity and the patience for understanding. ~

XVI

◈

Getting to Neutrality Beyond Assumptions

Assumptions are commonplace in the mind of those that do not seek to question their personal experiences or information that is given to them by others. At times, assumptions are the easy path to thinking less and at other times, they spark fixations of feeling and discomfort. Assumptions are part of the illusions one may perceive about others and the world, which feed the stories we tell ourselves about a situation or person. Assumptions are inevitable. They offer us a sense of consistency in our expectations in order to feel less of a burden in "not knowing." They offer us a sense of empowerment in what we think we know about ourselves and/or others. Assumptions and biases often potentiate one another and offer a measure of internal substantiation for our beliefs. The path to understanding oneself, others, and situational experiences requires us to ask questions and then, be receptive and contemplative of the answers that arise. Deeper understandings and accuracy of perceived truths can only be reached when an individual moves beyond their biases and assumptions to a state of honest curiosity and neutrality.

The experiences an individual has in life build in belief structures from any level of understanding a person is willing and capable of bringing to those experiences. Some say, "Hindsight is 20-20", but this cliché does not apply only because one has come to a conclusion they feel was missed in the moment. "20-20 vision" requires accuracy of perception about those factual events that tend to become a simplified memory or conglomeration of many things we tell ourselves about the experience or person we shared it with. How much of what we believe is 20-20 can obscure deeper understandings and the inaccuracy of perception if it is led by the unacknowledged biases or assumptions one carried before the situation transpired or the defensive coping mechanisms an individual uses when conflicts occur. The mind is easily filled with thoughts that are nurtured by one's feelings. If objective questions for logic and reasoning are not a consistent part of understanding the origin and accuracy of one's emotions, assumptions and one-sidedness will prevail.

It is true that we begin our understanding of anything from the focus and reference point of self, but we cannot disregard the co-creation of an experience when it involves more than just us. We must admit to ourselves there are always the known and unknown attributes to the multi-dimensionality of human experience. Therefore, the perceptions and perspective of the others involved must be taken into account when weighing the conclusions for a conflict or misunderstanding. When assumptions and biases reign without consideration for how others involved perceive themselves or what happened in the playout of events, direct shame and blame tactics, passive aggression, rejection through disregard, and defamation of character through one-sided story-telling and gossip are common.

All these responses to conflict exemplify self-absorption in personal assumptions and biases. How do you handle disagreements when conflict occurs? Do you contemplate questions with neutral receptivity to deepen your understanding of the others involved? When what we perceive is always referenced from oneself, it is easy to take things personally and make an experience all about us. Assumptions can feed the experience of personal offense like wildfire, even when there is not actual evidence for it. The balance of understanding what is personal and impersonal can be revealed by choosing neutral observation. This deepens one's understanding beyond assumptions. Do you question the source and accuracy of your emotions based in the factual context of an event? If you request advice from others for ongoing conflict, do you attempt to accurately represent both sides of the story?

An individual must care about the integrity of their own feelings, thoughts, and conclusions to acknowledge the contextual facts of a situation that may be agreed upon but responded to differently by others involved. When integrity and transparency for all sides of a situation are valued, objectivity and receptivity to others initiates curiosity and thoughtful questions that strengthen opportunities to reach a more wholistic truth for each individual. Achieving conflict resolution when a situation involves more than oneself means all individuals have the opportunity to seek closure through a sense of shared power in responsibility for the outcome, including differences of perception that end in division. The highest goal of conflict resolution is harmony and healing through progressive understanding of self and other. This is a hard goal to reach if assumptions and biases from previous wounds and defense mechanisms, built through past experience, control one's responses. In any given moment, an individual can only be as truthful with others as they are with themselves. They can only share what they know of themselves based on the introspection they have cultivated in their life experiences, patterns of belief, and capacity for intention.

When navigating relationships and personal experience of the world, it is essential to understand that assumptions and expectations create contractual agreements. These contracts may be overtly stated or covertly operating from inherent wounds or ideals an individual carries in the construct of their psyche. Overt contracts are direct, honest, and clearly spoken intentions, beliefs, or expectations. Covert contracts may be witnessed in duplicitous behaviors, emotional reactivity without explanation, and feeling blindsided by expectations of self or from others through various forms of social punishment. How does it feel when someone holds you responsible for something you didn't know was expected of you? Do you communicate your needs and wants with requests before shaming and blaming others?

Learning to ask questions is how one gets beyond assumptions to neutrality. Refining one's understanding of the multi-dimensional human experience is the practice of mindful self-awareness. When assumptions become judgments about others, it is important to ask oneself if those judgments are in service to a pre-existing internal bias and vindicate a story that we often tell ourselves about how other people are or how we feel about ourselves in similar experiences. If so, we may have discovered a blind-spot that causes distortion in our perceptions of contextual reality. Blind-spots are biases or assumptions that operate covertly in the mind and tend to cause recurrent themes in life experiences that feel unresolved. Following the thread of thoughts and emotions that perpetuate similar stories in one's life narrative leads an individual back to the source of biases and assumptions casting a blind-spot. This source is often found in climactic life experiences and childhood conditioning that ripple out and return, again and again, for adherence and mimicry or for healing into a new path of belief, emotional response, and the stories we define ourselves by. When we cultivate new skills for communication, perceiving self, and a stronger co-creation in our personal narrative, we harness the integrity to honor others in their own process without needing to intimidate or dictate them with assumptions and biases that may not apply to them or the situation.

Choosing neutrality is the most honest approach to resolving a conflict when resolution is desired with others. The emotions one carries about the conflict are honest as well, but they are ours to sort out and interpret in order to clarify the accuracy and basis of our response. When storytelling begins to spin in the mind without the involvement of questions that can only be answered by others, it is helpful to refrain from misleading assumptions that may instigate more distortion and conflict. Surrendering to the unknowns and finding neutrality for receptivity brings the relief one is seeking through the mental antics of pre-concluding. Neutrality is its own state of interim conclusion before more is revealed and externally substantiated. Pre-conceived notions are an important part of how the mind formulates and catalogues understanding in any experience. They are a tool to ready an individual for resolving misunderstanding and/or requesting needs or wants that are coming up to be met.

When these notions lead to presumption and are used to target others, directly or indirectly, without evidence or input from various perspectives, assumptions are instilled more deeply into belief. Once instilled as belief, assumptions are more resistant to modification and the process of refining accuracy though curious contemplation when new information arrives. Assumptions activate resistance on all sides most often, due to the emotional distortion they create when they are inaccurate, which defaults into reduced interest or longer delays for resolution. Assumptions challenged about oneself or assumptions directed at us by another incite grappling with the entangled origins of those accurate or inaccurate beliefs. This is why neutrality and learning to ask questions with honest curiosity based in requests for transparency is a healthier approach to resolving concerns within oneself as well as concerns about others.

Trust in the accuracy and transparency of the information one is given or perceives within self has a key role in the practice of mindfulness, understanding experiences, and choices one makes on behalf of the knowns and unknowns. Trust is what builds an individual's capacity to navigate the many circumstances that arise in the journey of life. Although, assumptions and expectations may or may not evolve from an individual's trust in a particular belief. Neutrality requires trust as well. Trust that the answers will come, that more will be revealed. Not all beliefs are set in stone and assumptions do not automatically apply because an experience appears or feels emotionally similar to another in our initial perceptions of it. Internal and external substantiation fortifies trust when we are willing to let it be revealed to us, instead of dictating what we expect to become known. The adage on "self-fulfilling prophecy" carries wisdom where the fixation on our assumptions takes over. Then, the folly of illusion perpetuates one's life story because we are more focused on being right than being accurate and on dictating instead of co-creating. Neutrality is the way back to a curious mind, a fresh slate for the framework of trust to be rebuilt and persevere beyond pride's need to control. This path enables profound new discovery to enlighten a darkened soul.

- Be willing to identify and question assumptions as they arise about self, others, and situational experience. Seek out the un-

knowns to formulate questions and inspire deeper understanding.
Let the well of your emotions show you the source of their activa-
tion and the still-point required to allow healing solutions. ~

XVII

❦

The Keys to Communication

In a diverse society with many cultures and individual experiences that frame our language and behaviors from childhood, successful communication may feel challenging. Since every individual is a separate catalog of experiences and inherent emotional mapping, as well as the expression of numerous probabilities in their genetic code and neural development, finding keys for successful, healthy communication is essential for a sustainable relationship with others and society, as a whole. Learning ways to communicate that create higher outcomes for connection and less causes for disconnection benefits everyone. By putting the effort into learning key methods to communicate, one increases the odds of getting their needs met, expressing their true self, sharing power in relationships, and healing wounds perceived when disconnection feels imminent. The art of communication challenges everyone to be more mindful of how their actions and words align, as well as how these communications affect others in their delivery or withholding.

Keys to communication help an individual unlock the doors to greater thresholds of connection and intimacy. Understanding the self and what one chooses to express is imperative to practice intention and accountability, which cultivate clarity and trust with self and connection with others. The more impulsive an individual is, the less trustworthy they may be perceived. Impulsivity does not lend itself to reliable emotional security and sets up the expectation for unpredictability. Developing skills to slow down one's response to an experience and/or communication from another, enables the assessment of what one wants and how to express those needs or requests. Likewise, those who overthink their response or choose not to respond at all must acknowledge that the lack of immediate response is perceived differently by others and is still a form of communication. Waiting too long to respond sets up the expectation that there may never be one and begins the cycling of assumptions for self-resolution of an event or the cleaving of desire for any further communication. The timing expectation for a response may vary from individual to individual or incident to incident. It is always reasonable to communicate verbally what amount of time someone needs to respond, as well as the amount of time someone feels open to waiting for a response.

Relationships are built on communication styles. The experience of separation through a disconnect or conflict and the experience of belonging through agreement and compassionate connection are ruled by breakdowns or successes in communication styles. Building a bridge to understand one another, especially at the beginning of a relationship or when big challenges occur that may change the fabric of the bond, is the only way to nurture appreciation and respect for the connection. Throughout life, communication styles or the capacity to communicate changes, depending on biases created from previous experiences, impactful events that initiate deep emotional overwhelm, and/or brain and bodily changes as an individual ages or faces major health crises. When communications seem off or different it is important to ask someone what is causing them if you value the relationship and their wellbeing. Reacting aggressively, passive-aggressively, or avoiding them altogether are not expressions of care and respect for the other person or an expression of desire to create understanding. The former verbal and behavioral reactions shut down the flow of connection and block the path to understanding. When these are consistently the immediate approaches used when an individual is feeling a disconnect or separation, the bond in relationship is wounded repeatedly over time, weakening connection, trust, and loyalty even if the moment seemed resolved and relationship continues. This is because communication conditions others' expectations of us.

When we seek understanding and use our words to deliver intentional invitations and requests, we expand the power of our own emotional intelligence. When we share power in a relationship by letting each person have a voice and listen intentionally with an open mind and heart to what they have to say, we expand the emotional intelligence and intimacy of the relationship. Ensuring one's behaviors align with their words and intentions is how we further co-create trust and reliability that what we say is what we mean. If there is a dissymmetry in our behaviors after our stated truth or agreements, these will be noticed almost immediately, because humans are animals first. Animals are wired to watch and remember behaviors more than words. This is why children notice and many times mimic their parent's behaviors, regardless of whether their parents are verbally honest with them. The old adage "Do as I say, not as I do" seldom works. Words can have more power when an individual wants them to, such as when they want a fantasy and choose to override what they have witnessed in order to perpetuate their desires by negating their instincts. The beauty of love, alone, is not enough to ensure understanding, trust, and reliability. The definitions of who we are, the relationships we seek to create, and our perceptions of love unfold in diverse ways. This is why learning how to communicate most effectively is worth the effort, if one seeks fulfillment in love and connection with others. Words and behaviors must align if we want to be understood and respected. Words and behaviors are the pillars of the intentional bridges we co-create with others that seek interdependent relationships, intimacy, and trust.

The path of communication styles is a diverse network of similarities and differences but where they overlap supports the capacity for connection through learning and appreciating other individuals that on their own journey to understanding and communicating with themselves and others. Some individuals are capable of communicating with a wide variety of personality types because of the willingness to build a bridge and be a witness to others who meet life and relationship on very different terms. It is up to every individual to evaluate their own capacity and interest to connect with others that are different than them. Every individual has gifts to offer in connection and lessons to learn in communication. When disconnection and disagreement feel imminent, compassionate release can still be found. The skill of compassionate release requires intention, respect, and humility. Words or gestures that show appreciation, accountability, and acknowledgment offer healing release when they are able to be received. Sometimes, the receptivity to these offerings takes years but that is irrelevant. As long as the intention for accountability, acknowledgment, and appreciation is honest, the one who has given it is free to heal on their own, while releasing the other to heal in their own time, when and if they choose.

The keys to successful communication for connection are curiosity, transparency, respect, personal accountability, a willingness to understand when disconnection or conflict occurs, and compassion for what can or cannot be communicated or agreed upon. Words and behaviors must align to form a trustworthy foundation and self-reflection is necessary to assess this. Once we each acknowledge the gifts that we bring into the world to share with others in this mutual learning experience, we can harness our own personal power and expand our ability to express that wisdom. It is a choice of devotion to the authentic self and the wisdom one carries to share with others, every day, regardless of the trade-offs that come in the dance of relationship. No matter the connection or disconnection one feels to others at times, this personal power and wisdom should never be relinquished. It is meant to be expanded through the fine-tuning of our communication with self and the bridges of understanding we co-create with others.

~ Center yourself at the threshold of your mind's eye and open the door to your heart. Align and express yourself with authenticity and curiosity for the ways and wisdom of others. Choose humility and respect for the teachings of disconnection and fine-tune the language of mutual connection through compassionate communication. ~

XVIII

༄

The Pain of Separation &
The Joy of Belonging

From the time we are born to the moment we die, a sense of separation exists in our perceptions of self to others, the world, and something nameless beyond. Separation is the covert antagonist when one experiences a loss or death of another. Grief, sadness, resistance, confusion, and deep emptiness mark the expressions of perceived separation and reveal to us the desire and pleasure we value in the gifts of connection. Through connection with others and the world outside oneself, the joy of belonging becomes known. Feeling embraced and welcome for what one wants and has the capacity to share cultivates the experience of connection, while the success and endurance of connection validates an individual's trust that they belong beyond the pain of separation when it occurs. The pain of separation and the joy of belonging dictate the ebb and flow of one's emotional experience and how an individual constructs and deconstructs the mazelike projections of their psyche.

The hall of mirrors is a strong metaphor for the maze of thoughts and emotions an individual navigates within oneself. "Everywhere you go, there you are", or at least some part of you that is either conditioned or choosing to show up in response to information you are processing in the experience of yourself, as a part of life. The connection or disconnection an individual feels within ripples out to their relationships with others just as one's perceived connection or disconnection in each of these relationships ripples back into perceptions of oneself. Separation defines self from others and enables individual experience. This establishes the opportunity to refine how an individual connects or disconnects with others. It challenges an individual to be in service to their relationship with themselves and become a studious witness to how they navigate interactions with others and the world. Becoming the authentic self and establishing self-worth is a constant journey of mindful weighing, sorting, claiming, and releasing. Acknowledging the evidence of your integrity in your beliefs and actions, honoring one's emotional experience, and deepening into the methodical assessment of multifaceted perspectives for all involved, is essential to a healthy separation of self from others.

The desire to belong presents the impetus to seek out connection that nourishes and acknowledges your own value. What an individual perceives in their worthiness will affect the connections they choose to endure, as well as the conformity to that relationships' demands over time. It is essential to safeguard one's sense of worthiness and self by asking the questions "Does this person or community care about who I truly am? How much do I have to give up of my authentic self to feel like I belong? Am I relinquishing who I want to be or have always been, in order to avoid separation and maintain a sense of connection?

When an individual asks these questions, the weighing of trade-offs in what is gained and lost outside of self is juxtaposed with the gains and losses within oneself. This is a time when honoring the sacrifices and self-deferral one has chosen for the benefit of perceived belonging is the most responsible approach, regardless of the choice to continue or discontinue relationship. Self-love requires trust in self which requires honesty and accountability in the choices an individual makes as they navigate life and relationships. Understanding is the fruit of these experiences that casts light on more fulfilling paths in the maze of our minds and fortifies opened or closed doorways in one's heart.

The exploration of belonging and separation are a part of the journey to knowing oneself. The perception of one's value can be diminished or empowered in both, depending on the balance of honesty and authenticity with self. No matter how much we strive for connection and belonging, a sense of separation will always feel inevitable because of the diversity cultivated in each individual's sense of self. Yet, the feeling of connection is also persistent because of the reflections we bear witness to in others about the experiences of separation and belonging, connection and disconnection, hardship and success. The fabric of emotion, mutual existence on the earth, and interactions to meet basic needs for survival are the threads that will always connect us as humans.

The experience of separation or the experience of belonging may be tended and expanded in an individual's awareness, depending on the perceptions one holds most valuable for a sense of protection and security. Some believe that foregoing the joy of belonging prevents them from the pain of separation. Others believe belonging protects them from the experience of separation. Neither are absolute or true because they both exist inside each of us all the time. From the moment we are born we feel separation from our mother. We need her love and protection to feel safe and to teach us the joy of belonging. We build the experience of connection and belonging with our family unit and playmates by mimicking and sharing our thoughts and feelings which reveal our differences more and more over time. These differences challenge us to work harder to belong or to lean into feeling separate and alone. Our mother and our life cannot give back the sense of oneness we felt in the womb. It is not until death that we can return to the "unknown", the mysterious abyss of wholeness we were birthed from. An individual says yes to life and all its possibilities when they embrace the journey of separation and belonging.

Separation and belonging are neutral gatekeepers to one's emotional experience. It is up to us to explore the realms they keep. It is up to us to define and expand the potency of our individual and shared understandings in service to self-love, worthiness, and integrity with the core of our authentic self. Relationships will grow through connection and relationships will falter in times of disconnection, no matter what role they take on in an individual's life. The path to reconnection and belonging, from the conflict driving disconnection and the pain of separation, invites all of us to refine our capacity to build bridges where we feel divided. Where no bridge can be built, a boundary of separation will stand. The ability to honor our differences and perspectives is what defines healthy boundary from a detrimental wall. Walls do not serve the expansive awareness of self when they are made to reject understandings that are in service to the self and to all involved. Walls may serve self-protection but often obscure an individual's view of reality, beyond the biases of one's own mind. The psyche and the world are a perpetually changing landscape. The more walls someone raises, the easier it is to be trapped in the gaze of one's own mirrors. Healthy boundaries are flexible yet firm in their function. They allow an individual to receive what is in service to their deeper understandings without blocking others or the world completely out. Their elasticity allows us to explore their relevance to new connections or new phases of long-term relationships with a firmness that is founded in the protection of the authentic self we seek to share.

- Embrace the choice to explore the pain of separation and the joy of belonging. Expand your vision beyond the maze of your mind and listen deep to the heart's intuition. Rise above the walls within to sense the most direct path to honoring your authentic self. Learn how to build a bridge between your self-value and your value of others in order to refine the function of healthy boundaries in times of change. -

XIX

⎯⎯⎯

The Many Faces of Love

In our journey of life, we come to know many shades of love. These shades may have different faces as we or others embody them. When an individual takes on a role in relationship, the attributes of love unveil themselves through the course of that relationship. Where less intimate forms of love exist, deep appreciation is felt. This appreciation reveals itself in various exchanges with colleagues, acquaintances, and general community interactions. The closer the bond, the more deeply felt the love is. In all senses of love defined by a role, the conditionality of that role holds sway. The deepest and most expansive undercurrent of love is unconditional. This love is a deeply spiritual conversation and acknowledgment that "all is embraceable as a part of the whole". It is the love that drives creation and becomes most evident in the love of a parent for their child. Try as they may and wish as we might, no other face of love in other relationship roles will reach the potency of this profound love and creative force between parent and child.

Parent and child relationships vary in their experiences. The perception of love is highly dependent on what is given and what is not given by the parent to the child. Some parents do not have the emotional, mental, or physical capacity to be fully present for their child. When this occurs, a sense of wounding in the bond between parent and child blocks or diminishes the flow of unconditional love and trust. The perception of this has a ripple effect throughout the life narrative of experiences that the child feels challenged to grow through. A perpetual desire lingers deep in the creative fire of the heart to unearth unconditional love in the bond with another, as well as restore it with their parent. This is innate, no matter how hard one's upbringing was experienced or how much one sabotages the flow of love in their relationships with others. The soul wants to belong, to know it has a place where an abiding embrace exists.

An individual may seek this unconditional love from another family member, a close friend, a lover, or spouse. One may repeat patterns in relationship dynamics or roles they take on to work out the desire beneath to know love, in its greatest form. No matter how many other shades of love they interact with or embody, an individual will find discontent if their fixation on the seemingly intangible experience or reproduction of the parent/child devotion does not manifest. It is essential to consider relationship expectations, repetitive roles that play out without the desired outcome, and the sense of dependency an individual places on others as though they were like a parent or child.

The psychoanalysis about men seeking their mothers and women seeking their fathers in love relationship has become more common in conversations, today. The relevance of our initial imprinting of what masculine and feminine roles and love with them feels like reveals the seeds of expectation or rejection in the mind and heart.

Beyond these considerations of co-dependent and conditional relationships, exists a larger question of how to create interdependence and deeply compassionate love that is as close as one can get to the original power of unconditional love inherent in creation. When an individual chooses to heal the wounds they carry, more dimensions of the wound can be revealed for understanding of how it came about, how it is perpetuated, and what is beneficial to resolving that wound. There are many wounds in the journey of life and the invocations and transformation of love. The most definable shades of love appear in the faces of those that represent our greatest wounds, in the way they were inflicted, and those that bring offerings to our dreams for healing resolve.

When an individual establishes self-authority and chooses honorable transparency to have integrity with the authentic self, they are invoking unconditional self-love. This invocation activates the will to understand and heal the mental, emotional, and spiritual wounds they carry. Throughout the alchemical journey to discover the authentic self, an individual cultivates proficiency in directing the experiences of one's personal narrative. This achievement is like unfolding a quilt with many interwoven seams that can be seen and felt. It takes a long time for some sections and quick completion for others. When it is large enough and many life experiences have formed it, it can be observed objectively and wrapped around oneself with appreciation for the multifaceted value and function it serves. To see it this way, with compassionate self-regard, is to return to the teaching of unconditional love that creation exhibits and the inner child craves. An individual can do this at any time in their life, if they seek harmony with the inner child and their relationships in the external world. You are the face of love in all its shades and you hold the potential to heal your wounds with intention, to offer accountability and transparency to others, to open healing opportunities for them, and prevent inflicting further wounds.

When we become clearer about how to carry expectations for oneself, others, and relationships, as well as cultivate healthy communication with invitations and requests, we harness the fluidity of loving exchange. By keeping the flow of love open, one is committed to releasing resentments, judgments, and inaccurate projections from our own imprinting onto those we seek to share life with. Even when one decides it no longer feels healthy to share life with someone, the way we find resolve alone and/or together reveals the shade of love we are experiencing within our own capacity. Even in endings, the flow of love for the exchange is most nourishing when kept open with healthy boundary. This approach to love is refined through co-creation and ripples out through our relationships to the degrees of connection that intertwine the fates of many others in society. Considering the shades of love experienced in an individual's life can clarify the projections one has placed on others that they identify as faces of love. It can also reveal deep truths that were unseen about the love others have offered to us that we could not receive or reciprocate at that time.

Assessing one's capacity for returning and sharing love with themselves and others is possibly the most important measure of an individual's life story. The constant flow of creation is embodied within and all around us. This persistent call resonates deep in the heart and travels the seams of one's identity, all the way back to the spark of one's inner child when it was dancing in the starlight before entering the mother's womb.

- Salute the dawn of creation in your burning heart. Embrace the wounds in your knowing field and sense the roots of unconditional love to discover a path for resolve. Honor the potency in the faces of love you share life with and cherish the spark of your inner child. Reveal the shade of love that you embody, unfolding your quilt to share that warmth with others. ~

XX

❦

Seeking Innocence Through Veils of Illusion

What is innocence? The supreme depiction of innocence is most often applied to children. From the helplessness and full dependence of an infant to the curious naivete of adolescents, "adults" sanction mistakes, downplay emotional reactivity, and nurture fantasies to maintain the longevity of perceived innocence. Caring adults safeguard children from the suffering found in the world outside the one they seek to contain them in. At every turn, loving parents seek to soften their experience of pain, discomfort, and challenging lessons believed to be more pertinent at a later stage of development. The guidance of a loving parent may offer examples of coping mechanisms, soothing affection for support, and seeds of consideration to help understanding or appeasement as the child expands their experience of self, others, and their world. As an adult, are we ever truly innocent or do we create the illusion of innocence because we seek to relieve ourselves of responsibility? When a child becomes what is perceived as an "adult", they are offered less room for mistakes, emotional outbursts, and getting lost in fantasies. This does not mean the child dissolves and is now only an adult. The child is held more inward, less on the surface, with the adult role in place as the overseer of one's life. Overtime, one's playful and curious inner child may be silenced by compensations for challenging life experiences to the point of feeling lost, yet the essence of it is apparent each time one comes up against the question of innocence, the opportunity to linger in fantasy, and the impulse for denying responsibility.

Re-discovering, nurturing, and healing one's inner child is an essential component of feeling whole, healthy, and enthusiastic to be in the world. Honoring the child within us opens a path back to self-love, self-forgiveness, and acceptance of what we are learning in the experiences of our lives. It allows the creative mind to be in an open state of discovery and adaptability for the intrigue of one's effects on the world where their life stories unfold. These beneficial aspects of a thriving inner child are supported in balanced companionship with an individual's adult sense of authority. The adult authority helps navigate the flow of creativity into strategic outcomes, while maintaining a conscientiousness of self and others in order to achieve the most productive outcomes in relationships and society. Caring for oneself and others is a primary lesson in achieving a healthy sense of leadership and authority, required to make adult decisions that involve more complex collaboration with others over time. This is evident in teamwork in college, career settings, long term relationships whether friendship or romantic, and building a family of your own.

Some children have experiences at a young age that push them into roles with more authority for themselves and/or the family.

Most often, the imprinted concept of authority in an individual's psyche is governed by a parent or adult that was most influential in their childhood. When these factors are holding sway over a healthy relationship with one's inner child as they grow into their adult authority, attentiveness to healing and re-educating the child self through mindfulness and introspection is a powerful way to refine how an individual expresses their authority with themselves, how they care for others, and how they understand the significance of innocence and responsibility. Innocence and responsibility are deeply rooted in the personas of the "Judge" and the "Victim" that present in the way one talks to themselves. This same judge and victim mentality, that leads within an individual's perception of self, affects the way they evaluate their experiences with others which may cause further distortion and illusion that are detrimental to an individual's relationship to oneself and others. If an individual lives from the primary state of the judge or the victim mentality, power struggles and poor resolve will dominate the stories of their life.

The "Judge" and the "Victim" personas govern the perceptions of guilt and innocence, of authority and whimsy, and of power and powerlessness. These personas distort the context and factual evidence of experience, as well as negate the conscientiousness of a balanced accountability with self that displaces the focus of blame on another or intensely upon themselves. The judge mentality may condemn and conflate toxic shame within self that mires a loving orientation to one's inner child and their opportunity to learn instead of shutting down through self-rejection. Likewise, the victim mentality panders to the inner child's mistaken choices and naivete, protecting themselves from achieving a healthy sense of adult authority. Denial, projection, and lying combine to uphold the veils of illusion that are spun when seeking innocence without honest assessments of an experience. These tactics of the mind play out from fear, incited by the judge or victim roles that dominate within an individual's relationship with their inner child and adult authority. Sometimes, these tactics were taught to us through mimicking another. Sometimes, they were learned through trial and error as coping mechanisms when life seemed too intense for the fragility of our childlike essence.

Coping mechanisms are often chosen to achieve a sense of redemption from the choices one makes, yet our unhealed wounds are re-experienced, again and again, when that redemption is falsified. Self-perpetuating chaotic and painful experiences is a pattern of fixation when an individual is seeking some offering of redemption that can only be truly found in deeper understanding of the self and one's role through the choices they make within those experiences. No one wants to feel guilty. This is the challenge every individual faces when accepting accountability for their choices, for their awareness or ignorance, and for the responsibility that comes with standing in your own power to affect resolve in an experience. The most common unhealthy ways of dealing with guilt are avoidance and disregard of responsibility to self, or the situation, and by placing blame on others. Self-righteous attitudes that demand consequence, without acknowledging their own involvement in the outcomes of a situation, are based in distortions that reveal long held wounds in the inner child that are demanding attention. Righteousness is distinctly different than self-righteousness. This is discerned by the evidence of firm boundaries that honor the integrity with self, sustained compassion for others, and an individual's capacity to wield their own power to reach healing resolve within themselves.

At a soul resonance level, we are all innocent. We are innocent and not held to any standard and we are free to play, sense, and learn from the essence of our inner child as we navigate what it means to exist, at all. The egoic mind and the imprints of the authorities that came before us are what construct concepts of right and wrong, standards to be met, and echoes of possibility to be followed. It's all theory. It's an abstract collection of known and unknowns in volumes of books that share the life stories of others. There is a natural cause and effect and there are consequences to be learned from our choices, but many of them are illusions propped up by ourselves or others in the search for meaning. These beliefs and consequences act as a catalyst for direction in the learning process that shapes one's sense of adult authority and the concept of one's inner child as a perceived or chosen identity. There are systems constructed of meaning and symbolism that we feel called to following, whether we are born into them, find them at some transformational point in life, or are attached to them because of intense emotional experiences that we are still learning to process. To be human in a society with others is to agree to the stated or unstated structures of belief, in some loose or stringent way, about what is acceptable or unacceptable in our behaviors. Individual relationships may establish their own agreements for what is acceptable or unacceptable, according to the roles, needs, wants, historical imprints, and explorations of belief for those involved. Therefore, communication of these expectations and beliefs is essential in order to move beyond initial or pervasive assumptions that may not be met, which then cause unnecessary dissonance within self or conflict with another. The perceptions of karma and fate all come with consequences perceived as positive or negative. We are the ones who attach meaning and the relevance of consequences to what we have or have not done in the course of our life chapters. We live from those theories because they act as a guide to our soul's resonance as it leads with patient witnessing in the background of the life cycles and patterns one is working to discover, heal, achieve, and surrender. The soul is the ultimate authority beyond the many divisions of self that can be defined in the psyche. It is where all of them are unified in the simplicity of "I am" and "It is what it is."

The inner child can be reactive, petulant, naïve, and demanding. It can be hidden, fearful, distrusting, and hypersensitive to others. Yet, it is also playful, loving, curious, and imaginative. It is comedic, enthusiastic, empathic, and opportunistic. The adult authority can be protective, instructive, logical, and emotionally contained. It can be loving, supportive, collaborative, and conscientious. Yet, it can be controlling, unforgiving, neglectful, and stubborn. It can be silencing, emotionally removed, enabling, and excessively responsible. Both of these aspects of one's psyche must find balance through conversation and the will to heal for the sake of fulfilling companionship with self. This companionship with oneself safeguards the return of an individual to the power of their own identity through self-love and wisdom beyond conflicts and hardship. What is your relationship like to yourself? Witnessing the dialogue within to heal the patterns that lack resolve is the first step to harnessing your power and to affecting perceptions of yourself, as well as interactions with others, that co-create your life story. Your life story is your legacy. Let it be one of new discoveries and deep healing in the wounds of the past. Let it be a dance of balanced accomplishments led by your inner child and adult authority. Through intentional living and the will to grow one can embody the potency of their authentic self, which has the power to strengthen endurance in compassion and adaptability for the changing landscapes of life.

~ Establish awareness of your inner dialogue. Embrace your inner child with compassion. Lighten the hand of self-authority with seeds of wisdom and tend the garden together with laughter, dedication, and mutual responsibility. Lay down in the dreams of tomorrow and wake up with many healed yesterdays, to be fully present in the choices you make today. ~

XXI

❦

Seeking Harmony to Liberate the Soul

In a world of diversity, the cascade of emotions and thoughts we each experience challenges our capacity to find harmony within oneself and with others. The pressure to explore and discern this harmony for fulfilling outcomes can ignite further reactivity of emotion or avoidance of the challenges one faces, in order to obtain a sense of relief or freedom. While the mix of instinctual and imprinted emotional responses arise with a stream of egoic thoughts to protect oneself and have power over the situation, the soul of our truest self is attempting to find a matching resonance for a collaborative outcome that nourishes or appeases the experience for all involved. A sense of honest liberation from any experience, emotional cycling, or thought fixation is only discovered in the harmony of the soul's resonance. The voice of a soul will not be denied. It runs deeper than emotion and dictates more than the power of one's thought. When the resonance for harmony is achieved, the transformation of life patterns, the healing of woundedness, and the wisdom to uphold one's power within enable the experience of fulfillment in the pursuit of happiness.

Resonance is a powerful governor in the regulation of all life. It is operating in the background of everything at all times. Every living thing has its own collection of sounds and vibration, humming its own song. We each mirror and share notes of this song in the origin of our species DNA and in congruence with the earth's overarching requirements to sustain life. We are a cacophony of tones striving to perpetuate and contain "vitality." When the pulse in our vessels and the timing of our neuron transmissions are disrupted or change, a breakdown in our strength and clarity is inevitable. Emotions and thoughts carry the power of resonance and the same vulnerability to discordance many times a day, let alone a lifetime. Harmonizing the discord within the mental, emotional, and physical bodies is an active choice that underlies the experience of being human. As one expands their self-awareness and their consciousness of resonance, they align with the essence of their soul's harmonic blueprint. This blueprint is a guidelight for how to re-balance and fortify one's sense of unity, clarity, and contentment when conflict creates dis-harmony or disconnection within self.

Liberation is closely associated to harmonic resonance. There is an awareness of fluidity, ease, and uplifting invitation to be one with that sensation. The quietude of the mind and the receptivity of the heart is a marked attribute in the most supreme moments of perceived harmony. As the vibration of thoughts and emotion transform beyond the dissonance of conflict, the pressure releases, one's breath expands, then exhales like a bird taking flight, circling back to land and lift off, again and again. This is the sensation of fulfillment that occurs when conflicts are resolved, wounds are healed, and the alignment with one's soul resonance is in harmony. It is the peace symbolized by the white dove and the power to rule oneself from the soul's wisdom associated with the eagle in spiritual practices. A false sense of liberation may come through the dance of the egoic self when an individual does not want to realize the illusions they create or are attracted to. This sense of freedom from pressure lacks the grounding cord of soul resonance and is often short lived. The story that perpetuates in the fall out of illusion, when open or covert expectations are not met, is evidence of the egoic self dictating one's experience. Attuning to the soul's resonance is a refinement process in conversation with the egoic self. This requires attentiveness with curiosity to discern which part of self is operating in the hierarchy of their life choices.

Conflict resolution, co-creating harmony, and honoring one's power within are all necessary for a sense of perceived justice that advocates for the mind and the heart. Justice is not only about logic and not only about emotional vindication. Weighing the scales of any situation, whether inspiring or challenging, is heavily dependent on the resonance the one who is weighing those scales is attuned to. Some are attached to their mental deductions, while others lean into their emotional imprints, but accuracy requires that these aspects of egoic self find balance and allow the potency of what the soul is asking for to be the overseer and conductor that harmonizes the symphony of experiential perceptions. Attuning to the requests of one's soul blueprint opens a path to a web of understanding that benefits an individual's developmental journey, as well as any others affected by the choices they make from a place of healthy empowerment and accountability on that journey. That web of understanding is interwoven in the background of all our life stories and is the origin of the elements that repeat themselves in scales of harmony or discord.

Discord is draining. It scatters one's energy and focus toward unproductive, distracting thoughts or emotional overwhelm. Discord is powerful in calling out the shadow aspects of the egoic self and pulling one deeper into distortion, away from their soul's harmonic resonance. If prolonged, this may become the experience of "losing oneself", of feeling cast out from life or one's dreams, and martyring oneself in the belief of powerlessness. The sensations of dissonance and harmony are natural attributes of the duality in life and the soul's journey to knowing itself. It is the choice to follow or stay in dissonance or harmony that is up to us. When dissonance occurs or perpetuates, the most direct way to attaining peace or harmony is to trust the power of free will you carry within. This power can be used to instigate further dissonance or suppression of the soul's resonance, that leads to dis-integration of heart and mind inevitably, or it may be used to re-establish a center for balance and clarification of how to conduct oneself with the intention of harmonization. Harmonization may not be matching the exact tone of another or a situation. It is often a complementary tone that flows with or strengthens the tone of another or a situation. It may be a choice to welcome the song you are creating with another back to a place of harmony, if they are willing to meet you in that intentional effort, as well.

Musical ensembles are defined by scales and how they resonate together. The same is true of the soul and therefore the mind and heart when accordance is discovered and chosen. No one can take your power from you or diminish the capacity of your soul. It is an illusion that you or anyone else is ever fully in control of another at the soul level. Any moment of discord or dissonance is an opportunity to maintain the strength of one's soul resonance and to offer the same respect to others for honoring their soul's resonance.

When intentional effort to harmonize is resisted or denied, individuals are no longer creating together. They are playing out the sounds of their own song, no longer honoring the journey of sharing resonance in unity. Sometimes, this is the best approach to reach harmony with soul resonance for both the individuals, whether immediate or eventual. Many times, the experience of breaking away for solo focus on oneself and the way one seeks to align with their soul resonance in a relationship, situation, or life chapter is pivotal in finding the most potent notes of wisdom required for the future unfolding soundtrack in their soul's journey.

Every relationship has its own unified soul resonance to manifest, at all. This includes all roles played out through connections with others in family, romance, friendship, work or school, and communities we generally interact in. When the soul resonance of a relationship is ignored, the relationship begins to dis-integrate, showing signs of conflict and disconnection. It is common for most to choose oneself first and then, perhaps consider the other's experience, but attuning to the soul resonance they share and what this is asking in the relationship to maintain balance or perpetuation is often ignored or unheard. The capacity to honor each other as equals is the first step toward harmonizing and balancing perceived power struggles. Having accountability for the choices one makes in how they wield their power is essential for each individual involved in order to feel the strength and clarity of truth within and in the outcomes of those actions through their involvement. Harmony within self or within relationship cannot be found without personal accountability and consolidation of personal power. Discernment for where the resonance is faltering and collaborative considerations for the fulfillment of self and others involved then opens the path for liberation through healing and continued co-creation, ideally. If complementary collaboration or harmony in agreement cannot be found, acknowledging the completion of a shared song is also a powerful moment of liberation. How we end the call and response of a shared experience, with respect to balance of power and honoring self or others involved, creates an echo effect in future endeavors and songs we share with others because of how we carry it on within ourselves. The song is officially over when the story does not repeat itself in the mind and heart with lingering intensity. This includes the subtle pressure that amplifies as an imprint when a similar experience invokes the memory of other shared songs in our life stories.

The soundtrack to one's life can be replayed again and again, as edits, reprises, covers, and homages. This is the nature of soul resonance and the work of finding liberation through harmonizing all aspects of self within and with those we co-create with. Taking active steps to quiet the mind's logic and quench the heart's emotion, in order to listen and feel more deeply to the scales set forth by the soul, honors the potency of one's authentic self. When allowed, this authentic resonance guides how and what one manifests in the outcomes of experience. Fortifying outcomes that consolidate trust in our own power and precision for balanced justice, that are in alignment with the soul, refine one's capacity to feel nourished and share that strength in wholeness with the world.

~ Seek out the resonance of your soul when dissonance disrupts your vibe. Balance the scales of the heart and mind when truth comes to be weighed. Emotional intelligence is the chanting wisdom deep within. Embrace your own potency to activate the alchemy in songs calling for harmony to liberate and redefine the patterns of your own life stories. ~

XXII

꧁

Symbolism, Synchronicity, and Purpose

In the journey of human consciousness, we are driven to ascribe meaning, correlation, and application from objects, events, and interactions in the world. The human mind negotiates decisions through the lens of symbolism in a kaleidoscope of orchestrated timing that reaches into the abstract field of purpose. The depth of one's understanding constructs the view and opens the doors of perception with every new piece of collectable information. The capacity for witnessing new symbolic elements and factors in the context of their synchronicity expands an individual's conscientiousness, while fortifying attention to meaning and value in life as a whole. This relationship between symbolism and value is electromagnetic, a powerful force affecting the hands of time interdependently as history unfolds for review. Symbolism, synchronicity, and purpose are like the 3 Fates in Greek mythology, inextricable from the past, present, and future.

Symbolism, synchronicity, and purpose are malleable and transformative to the sentience of our being. The resonance of one's soul echoes like a siren for attention, lurking in the fog of our hunt for security in a sense of meaning. It is not easy to live a life without meaning or purpose. It is not easy to live a life completely detached from symbolism and relevance because the attempts to free oneself from these inherent urges in the experience of existence creates dullness and de-motivation, resulting from inertia. The illusion of living a life without meaning is itself an act of puppeteering, requiring the use of language and plot lines which are then masqueraded as meaning "without meaning." The illusion is only sustainable by the art of hyper-focused attention on a lack of meaning that ignores the pursuit of purpose. The disregard for any new information to challenge this perception creates a time loop of re-enforcing experiences dictated by one's emotional temperament that thickens the fog of a mind and obscures opportunities to expand conscious awareness. A similar result occurs in any fixation, no matter how light or dark, when the need to control life according to how one feels compelled to confine the experience of meaning, supercedes the humility of being a witness and co-creator of it. "Spiritual bypassing" is another experiential compensation for what may feel hard to acknowledge and deepen understanding in, relating to alternate views of what we call "reality." The persistent need to control meaning is draining in comparison to witnessing and considering the possibilities of meaning, which directly affect the relevance of value and purpose in a sense of meaning to that individual. This is because of the resistance required each time new information presents for an individual's awareness to expand and receive it.

The willingness to witness, consider, and correlate meaning is directly related to the underlying sense of purpose one feels within their own existence and the life they are living. The cumulative effect of valuation in meaning and purpose nourishes and sustains an individual's attention to what they manifest or strive to achieve. The way we attach meaning to symbolism draws a roadmap to the goals one sets and encourages the searching nature of the mind and heart to embrace the process of engagement between oneself and the world. This is required for goal achievement. This roadmap may have many twists and turns, doubling back on itself, along with leaps and bounds as we embrace the journey to understanding oneself, the story we are taking part in, and fortifying meaning in alignment with one's soul resonance. What once had meaning or perpetuated as a symbol in one's life may offer a sense of freedom once it is perceived differently or no longer relevant. Likewise, a loss of meaning an individual held great value for may feel overwhelming and incite the experience of suffering. They are both signs of transformation, an alchemical process of re-arranging elements to produce a new form or slate in order to evolve the awareness of self.

The synchronicity of experiences, witnessed symbolism, and formulating perceptions of meaning is the foundation that enables an alchemical transformation in the productivity of purpose. "Timing is everything," we say. Yet, "Time does not exist" is another perception of meaning ascribed to time. The parameters of time are what construct it, not time itself. The witness is an imperative component to the meaning of time. It is synchronicity that stands in solidarity, generating the parameters of time. Synchronicity is the equation we can choose to see in the background of the matrix we experience existence within. The function of events, acting in concert with the witness, and the viewable lens of symbolism in each moment is where the magic and mystery play their sleight of hand. Sometimes they reveal the illusion and other times they play it forward in a grander symphony of events, emotions, thoughts, echoes of meaning, displacement and refinement of values, and moments of certainty or curiosity that affect the choices we make. It is up to us to keep the doors of perception open, to be committed to understanding the relationships that synchronicity presents for witnessing. Turning one's attention to the considerations of synchronicity expands self-awareness and consciousness as a whole.

If we are the authors and co-creators of our lives, then becoming a scribe in the documentation, sorting, and reviewing of notable events, symbols, messages, and personal conclusions is a powerful practice. Journaling is like drawing a roadmap for the self. It enhances retainment of memories and knowledge. It acts as a reference for the review of feelings and thoughts still working up to the surface for correlation and relevance to momentary impulses and short or long-term coping mechanisms. Scrapbooking and art collage mixed with free writing and sketching are also forms of healing catharsis and reviewable outlets that expand self-awareness. Your own willingness to connect with yourself in this way is evident of the friendship, love, and wisdom you have the power to feel with yourself and your negotiations in life choices. Witnessing your own stream of consciousness can reveal many patterns of fixation and ways of being that effect the narrative your authentic self seeks to align for fulfillment.

Honoring what is most meaningful to you in the development of your character, how you share your energy with others, and what you seek to create that fulfills the calling within requires devotion to mindfulness and precision. No one else can tell you what is more meaningful or valuable to your experience. This must be discerned within and cultivated in the change of seasons that define the landscapes you traverse in the personal and collective realm of human consciousness.

The seeds of life generate the flowers that cast off their petals to ripen the fruit of their labors. This fruit decays to disperse its seeds beneath dark fertile soils. The alchemy of synchronicity procures the birth and endurance of purpose over many seasons in the body, mind, heart, and spirit. The meaning of existence serves itself. Those who honor the value of it must tend to its perpetuation with humility and receptivity for its evolution throughout time and relativity.

- Attune your vision to the kaleidoscope of possibility and refine the lens to sharpen understanding. Engage with time in a dance of synchronicity to discern the wisdom of alchemy and feel the merit of each transformation inscribed in the story of your authentic self. ~

Healing Mantras

For Everyday Experiences

Healing and empowering affirmations that may be repeated within or spoken aloud in order to attune your heart and mind to a harmonic resonance and shift patterns in thoughts and behaviors when challenges or initiations occur in your life story.

An Invocation of Gratitude

"I awake with vitality
in my veins.
I breathe with inspiration
in my lungs.
I embrace the dance
of color and form in the world
around me.
For every teaching I am fulfilled
with Gratitude."

Mantra for Curiosity

"I feel the call,
I hear the whisper-
of questions in the deep.
Every moment- a sea of treasures
for my resolve and delight."

Mantra for Confidence

"I am Strong
I am Whole
I am Love
and I will always
Be Enough."

Mantra for Patience

"The Light of Gratitude
surrounds and fills me.
I am at peace
with all that is in this moment.
Everything in its right time and place."

Mantra for Compassion

"I Honor you
I Honor me
with Love and Acceptance
for what is mine
and what is yours.
I seek the path of understanding."

Mantra for Humility

"I Honor you
I Honor me
with gratitude for these
teachings unfolding
and the ways of the
Great Mystery."

Mantra for Release & Resolve

"I define the borders and boundaries
of my emotional self.
I release the attachments and projections
of emotions and thoughts that are not mine.
I resolve the imprints in this moment
and beyond- that block, deter, distort, and compel
that do not serve my authentic self.
I am receptive to the highest truth
for benevolent fulfillment and
I invite in creative solutions
in alignment and harmony
for all involved."

Mantra for Resilience

"My bones are of the Mountain.
My heart is of the Sea.
My mind is quick as Fire.
My spirit Crystalline.
I am Resilient. I am Whole
and I will always Be."

Mantra for Sustainability

"I am capable because
Thoughtfulness becomes Efficiency,
Resourcefulness reveals Abundance,
Creativity perpetuates Sustainability,

and I am nourished because
I choose Effort diligently."

Mantra for Rebirth

"I stand in the night
and face the sun.
I rise in the day
and face the moon.
This forge of light within {me}
melts the past into future.
Transforming this vessel
of consciousness for Rebirth,
I am awake."

Mantra for Humanity

"It is my nature to create.
It is my nature to witness and learn.
It is within my grasp to improve and
within my attention to seek harmony and truth."

Mantra for Transcendence

"Rainbows laugh
in the face of this storm.
Become one with your light heart
to weather all doubts that are born."

Mantra for Collective Evolution

"Exhilarating,
Contemplating,
Integrating-
to Magnify,
Refine,
Communicate,
Share-
Ingenuity with All."

Mantra for Decisiveness

"Grounding into the earth
to feel my own nature,
I sense the pivot for direction.
Leaning into the vibration
for my highest good
and what may serve all involved,
I choose....
(Insert options here and feel the
strongest resonance guide you
toward a decision)...."

Mantra for Sacred Connection

"I honor the wisdom of my own heart.
I am receptive to the truth of others
and maintain healthy objectivity

for the protection of my own core values.

The well within me only deepens
when I choose integrity as a mirror
with myself and others.

I embrace the path of knowing
and sharing from my Authentic voice
to create sacred connection
in the journey of life."

Mantra for Precision

"I anticipate all possibilities
revealed to me and
unknown to me.

I align the impulses of my body, heart,
and mind with patience.

I keep my senses keen,
letting loose the arrow
to meet my mark
with elegant precision."

Mantra for Accountability

"I choose self-awareness
with each perceived failure or conflict.

I acknowledge the power
of all actions and statements,
whether intentional or unintentional,
that affect the outcomes in every moment.

I seek to refine my skills and behaviors
to create opportunities for healing
and mutual respect.

I embrace honorable transparency
to have integrity with myself and others."

Invocation of Power Mantra

"With honor and confidence
I choose how to use my power wisely.

I question my own motives
and seek the most harmonic outcome
in all circumstances.

With patience and clarity
I wield the power of intention for precision.

I stay alert to others
who seek to use their power against me
or to take my power from me.

I call back any and all power I have given
knowingly or unknowingly
to restore the well of my being."

Parting the Veils Mantra

"With courage, I will peel
back the layers of my own psyche.

With honesty, I will unveil the meaning
of my behaviors and choices.

With clarity, I will deconstruct
all imprints and programming
that do not align in the now

to share the truest nature of
my authentic self with the world."

Invocation for Karmic Resolution

"With humility, I acknowledge
the power of cause and effect
including the ripple effect of my choices.

When I feel the struggle of conflict and hardship
I seek the most complete solution.
I empower myself to heal and transform
all karmic debt or contracts as they become known to me.

I am a sovereign being who respects all sovereign beings.
I hold myself accountable for what I have the power to
change, to clutch, to end, and to rebirth."

Acknowledgment of Self-Authority

"I seek the will of sovereignty
and cultivate trust with my inner authority.

I release the perception that
anyone else has power over me.

I have the power to dream in my own authority.
No matter what I have been told or not told,
what has been forced upon me or what has never been given.

When I activate my own authority, the power to manifest
my true nature is confirmed to me.

I maintain openness and adaptability
to co-creating with the authority of others."

Mantra To Embrace Love in all its Forms

"The sweet satisfaction is mine
to explore and share love.
The power of love grows inside
with every victory and every loss.
For every face of love I have seen,
I say Thankyou, for teaching me.
Thankyou for loving me the way you know how.
I will honor that seed in the truth of your love
and I will hold gratitude for the love that I am."

Communication For Connection Mantra

"I want to hear the truth of your perceptions.
I want to acknowledge the power and strengths
I see in you.
I want to be seen and heard in the way I seek
to connect with you.
I will share my clearest understandings and
ask for what I need.
I will hold the door open to meet you and
invite the will of our highest harmony."

Honoring the Emotional Experience Mantra

"I embrace the alchemy of emotion
expanding my heart and soul.
I will reach into the well and
discern my deepest treasures.
Through the sensation of catharsis
I will hold up a mirror and reveal
truth beyond distortion.
I choose to live from the power
and wisdom of my heart
to honor my soul and to
unlock the maze in my mind."

Mantra for Neutralizing Assumptions

"When I feel conviction, I step back
and observe the evidence.

When I feel the call to assert my truth,
I acknowledge what purpose
this act is in service to.
I seek the center of conflicting truths for understanding
and cast out baseless assumptions,
programmed reactions, and defensive projections.
I choose balance beyond extremes
and have the courage to refine my beliefs
or bias with curiosity and respect for
the diversities of perspective."

Releasing Distortion Mantra

"I listen deep to the cry of my inner child,
and embrace the struggle to understand
myself, others, and the world.

I listen with the strength of a gentle parent
who knows best how to guide me and love me
in the structures I learn to create,
in order to nurture myself and others.

I feel the charge of my emotions
and the scatter of my thoughts.
I see a path to growth when I center myself
and accept a balanced sense of accountability
for the outcomes of my impulses and decisions.

I embrace the innocence of my soul
and remain open to learning how to dance
gracefully with my inner child and adult authority."

Mantra for Liberation & Harmony

"I embrace the symphony of my soul
and reflect in the resonance beneath
my thoughts and emotions.

I align with my highest sense of self
and seek harmony in all my endeavors,
relationships, and interactions with the world.

I trust in my own power to make choices
that tend to the healing of wounds I carry
and bring synchrony to any discord that arises
in the soundtrack I am creating for my life."

A Mantra for "The Mattering"

"The rustle of leaves calls me to listen.
The sweet song of birds invites me to feel.
The soft pull of gravity reminds me I am home.

Every sound, every stillness is a doorway
that I may enter.
Every history, every presence is abundant
with meaning and purpose.

I am one with the dance of relativity
in a matrix of possibility.
My heart and mind are open
to witness "the mattering"
in an ever, expanding field of knowing."

CHECK OUT

THE WEIGHTED FEATHER

COMPANION WORKBOOK!

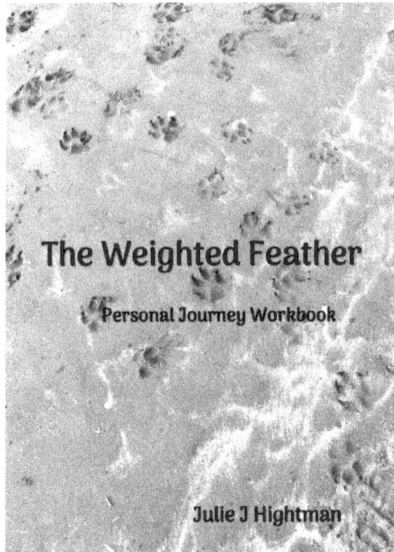

The Weighted Feather

Personal Journey Workbook

Julie J Hightman

EXPLORE YOUR OWN PERSONAL JOURNEY

THROUGH JOURNAL PROMPTS

AND CREATIVE EXERCISES!!

About the Author: Then to Now

Julie Hightman began her journey as a Holistic Healthcare Professional in 2004. Her focus on volunteering and treating addiction, abused women, veterans returning from war, and hospice have brought her many stories and experiences as a witness and facilitator of healing. Her offerings as a writer and an artist are another essential outlet for the passion and creativity she seeks to share with the world.

Author of "The Weighted Feather Vol. 1", the Poetry Collection "Seasons of Witnessing: Elemental Art & Poetry", and the Memoir "Why Birds Sing at Dawn: Embracing Death and Change as Transformation". Julie's message to the world is always one of curiosity, cathartic surrender, self-refinement, and the practice of savoring gratitude.

If you want to know more about her offerings or stay connected to new reflections and empowering practices, stay tuned via
www.FaizHealing.net
www.FaizHealing.com

www.ingramcontent.com/pod-product-compliance
Lightning Source LLC
Chambersburg PA
CBHW060234030426
42335CB00014B/1449